Stone Age Farming

Eco-Agriculture for the 21st century

by Alanna Moore

PythonPress
Australia

PYTHON PRESS
PO Box 929
Castlemaine
Vic. 3450
Australia.
Email: info@geomantica.com
Website: www.geomantica.com

Stone Age Farming -
Eco-Agriculture for the 21st Century
© Alanna Moore 2001.
ISBN: 0-646-41188-8.

Photos, diagrams, text and design by Alanna Moore, unless stated. Illustrations by Greg Smith. Thanks for editing and general assistance to Joy Finch, Tom Graves, Gil Robertson and Gary de Piazzi. Thanks to Junitta Vallak for photos and Steven Guth for 'Homodynamics' and photos.

Proudly produced in central Victoria.

Front and back covers: The tallest Round Tower in Ireland -
the leaning Tower of Kilmacduagh, county Galway,
with detail of its cyclopean stonework on back cover.

The opinions, advice and information in this book have not been provided at the request of any person, but are offered solely for information purposes. While the information contained herein has been formulated in good faith, the contents do not take into account all the factors that need to be considered before putting that information into practise. Accordingly, no person should rely on anything contained in this book as a substitute for specific advice.

CONTENTS

PART ONE: SOIL and SOUL

1.1 The Eco-Farming Imperative

Humankind is destroying our only home, planet Earth, at a frightening speed. Gobbling up forests and wilderness, which act as the Earth's lungs and cradles of water, in the name of forestry and farming. Abusing farm soils with excessive cultivation, grazing and chemical use. And an ever growing human population demands ever greater food production.

Farmers are under enormous pressure to produce food, with the strain of spiralling input costs and often falling product prices. (Consumers expect to pay much less for food these days, in proportion to income, than they did in earlier times.) With more than their fair share of chemical exposure, bankruptcy and suicide, the farmer is a dying breed. And the consumer is not far behind!

Dangers of Modern Agriculture

The majority of the world's arable land is affected by various forms of soil degradation. Insect and weed pests have developed increasing levels of resistance to chemical sprays. More and more chemicals are required, poisoning beneficial soil life, wildlife and farmers as well. Consumers sicken from eating and accumulating the chemical residuals. Modern agriculture, which evolved out of post-war-time chemical factories, brings a slow death to us all.

In Australia we have been applying inappropriate European farming methods to grow European plants on vastly older, worn out soils for far too long. Unlike their lush European counterparts, our soils are often low in minerals, microbes or organic matter, while rainfall is intermittent. Australian soils are desperately 'burn out', eroded and compacted, and suffer widespread rising salinity levels.

Erosion

Soil erosion has been documented since Plato lamented its effects in Greece some 2,300 years ago. The 'Fertile Crescent', that cradle of civilisation around the Tigris and Euphrates rivers, with its intensively irrigated agriculture is now all desert. A common outcome of de-foresting landscapes and irrigation farming.

We continue to lose topsoils at a frightening rate. Soil guru Dr Arden Anderson estimates the USA lost 50% of its farmland topsoil in the course of the 20th century. Every year, the U.S Soil Conservation Service estimates, American croplands lose over 3 billion tons of topsoil.[1] Do we really want our descendants to inherit nothing but a desert?

4

There are further downstream effects of erosion. Fly over the coast of Queensland and you'll see just where the topsoil ends up. At every river mouth - a giant fan of silt spreads out below you, choking and killing the precious living corals of the Great Barrier Reef.

Soils of low organic matter status are dangerously prone to erosion from wind and water, whereas organically rich soils, held together by organic matter, can absorb water readily, and rarely erode. So eco-agriculture can resolve this problem and is an imperative if society is to achieve sustainability of any kind.

Dryland salinity

Massive deforestation and subsequent agriculture has caused dryland soil salinity to become a major problem in parts of Australia. Some 15-20 billion trees have been cleared from the Murray–Darling basin alone, over the past 200 plus years. Without the deep rooted trees using up the underground water, ancient salt deposits are brought to the surface with rising water tables. This kills both native vegetation and crops, and ends up washed into the waterways, making fresh water undrinkable without expensive treatment. [2]

Worst affected are the Murray-Darling system and Western Australia's south western agricultural zone, the latter having some 80% of the country's most salt prone land. These are some of the most important agricultural regions in the country, with whole communities at risk. Not only farmland, but infrastructure, such as roads, the foundations of buildings and plumbing, is also threatened by rising salt.

Australia's first scientific assessment of dryland salinity levels was released late 2000. The audit says that 5.7 million hectare of land are at risk. This amounts to an area equivalent to 90% of Tasmania. Many rural towns are starting to have property damage from salt, while the three million people who rely on the rivers for drinking water are also threatened. A 1998 study estimated much lower future levels.

The CSIRO's Tom Hatton thinks that 30-50% of the Murray-Darling basin needs to be reafforested to help curb this problem. [2] As well as planting tree belts throughout farmland, techniques of eco-agriculture and soil remineralisation can also help - by reversing the processes of degradation.

Chemical Abuse

Chemical farming is like feeding junk food to kids. Sudden availability of NPK (nitrogen, phosphorus and potassium) gives a powerful dose of stimulants to the soil microbes. They party on until they keel over, having eaten out all available organic matter as a source of carbon in the process. Having burned out organic matter, the death of the microbe population results in a locking up of soil nutrients. The soil is dead, until the next dose of party food resurrects it. [3]

Nitrogen abuse of crops is common, with 50% of the water soluble form that's applied washing away from where it's needed. Residues of fertilisers and pesticides leach out into the waterways, joining the washed out topsoil to make modern agriculture a major threat to rivers. In tropical countries the problem is even worse, due to intense rainfall and accelerated erosion.

Many fertilisers contain toxic heavy metals, such as cadmium in superphosphate. The combination in soils of residual heavy metals, nitrates and other chemicals is a dangerous cocktail. Acids from chemicals dissolve humus in soils, and, while many plant diseases are controlled by antibiotics produced by natural soil bacteria and fungi that thrive around plant roots in the humus environment - these are killed off with chemical use.

Human health is often affected in agricultural areas. In a Mexican study it was found that kids who lived in a valley and drank water laced with pesticide residues, had developmental delays and were very aggressive, much more than a control group who lived up in the hills.

In a Minnesota study the children of pesticide applicators had increased levels of birth defects. Another study found that pesticide levels in people had accumulative effects and even with low levels there was increased incidence of cancers. [4]

In the US the EPA (Environment Protection Authority) estimates that pesticides contaminate the primary source of drinking water of over half that country's population. They also consider that 60% of all herbicides, 90% of fungicides and 30% of insecticides used there are carcinogenic, approved for use before stricter testing was mandatory. Californian farmers suffering pesticide poisoning have the highest rates of occupational illness in that state. There has been a tenfold increase in the use of pesticides in the U.S. between 1947 and '74, but crop losses to insects have doubled in that time, due to increasing levels of resistance to them. [1]

As well as being poisoned by modern agriculture, more and more studies are showing that diet is a major cause of many illnesses. The lack of proper nutrition inherent in foods is causing widespread malnutrition, and this reflects a very poor soil status. Poor nutrition is linked to a wide range of health and social problems.

Solutions?

Is there a solution to all these problems? Yes - many have already been successfully trialed, and they are not necessarily complicated or expensive. In fact few people can capitalise on such measures, so it is no wonder that little is heard of them. In a world of economic rationalism there's little money to be made in saving the environment and that endangered species the farmer, and thus little attention is given. Yet there is everything to be gained.

Farming needs to return back to being a wholesome and profitable activity. We can adopt eco-farming techniques that have proven successful in organic, biodynamic, and Low Input and Sustainable Agriculture (LISA) regimes. Permaculture principles can be applied to ensure appropriate land use and farm planning, with zones for the protection of native wildlife and water catchment.

Consumers will have to pay more - it's just a matter of setting priorities and putting health and wellbeing first. The premium prices paid for healthy food will make a saving on medical bills later on in life and probably save our rapidly eroding genetic status.

Ten years ago it might have been unthinkable, but the shift is happening. The supermarkets of Europe are going organic! The threat of 'mad cow disease' is making the German government demand that farming goes green, in the wake of an 80% drop in beef sales (in January 2001). England has seen a massive increase of land farmed organically - from 50,000 hectares in 1995 to 240,000 in April '99; while the EU had 3 million hectares in '98, up from 1.4 million in '95, according to NSW Greens Party policy literature (www.nsw.greens.org.au). Consumer power is pushing the necessary changes and shows how we can all be involved in ensuring human and planetary survival. Without the eco-consumer, eco-farmers cannot survive.

Ecological principles need to be applied as soon as possible to tackle soil degradation - while there's useable soil left. There is no need for endless government procrastination and scientific mastication on the subject. The answers are plain and proven. All we need is to have the will to begin, and to set goals, and work out strategies and time lines to achieve them.

Essential components of a healthy soil

For a truly healthy soil, with the capacity to produce food containing the optimal range of nutrients necessary for our health, we need to look holistically, for soil is a diverse ecosystem of great complexity. Ideal soil requires the following vital components:

- **Minerals** (easily obtained from rock dusts)

- **Energies** (sunlight, paramagnetism and other radiations)

- **Organic matter** (grown in situ, or applied as mulch or compost)

- **Microbes** (these make the minerals available to plants)

- **Water** (the purer and more energetic or natural – the better)

- **Air** (plants need CO_2 and good soil absorbs greenhouse gases)

Testing soil status

To begin the eco-growing approach it's ideal to start with a soil audit, testing for a range of required nutrients and their bio-availability.

The NPK fertiliser regime ignores the fact that humans need at least 20 other elements, even if they are only in tiny trace amounts, and that plants grow best when nutrients are released very slowly to them. Standard fertilisers tend to acidify soils and this itself is enough to lock away nutrients. Soils become dangerously imbalanced with NPK alone and plants sicken and attract pests.

Albrecht test

A soil which is properly mineralised and balanced, in relation to plant and human needs, however, grows crops with a maximum of quality and minimum of pest problems. Decades ago Dr Albrecht and his associates found that soil with 'perfect balance' has a pH of around 6.5 and with about 85% of its fertility holding capacity (CEC) filled with 3 key mineral elements - calcium, magnesium and potassium- in the optimum proportions of 70%, 12% and 3% respectively. This philosophy is followed by Brookside Laboratories in the USA, where many Australian farmers send their soil samples for testing, although this can also be done in Australia.

Reams test

Another type of soil testing of increasing popularity has been developed by Carey Reams, an American agronomist who further developed Albrecht's work. Reams realised that traditional soil testing did not give an accurate picture of the soil's actual fertility level. The Reams soil test was developed to reflect, in the test values, the characteristics actually observed in the field. Soil compaction and tilth; weed and pest problems; crop quality and yield; and the overall stability of soil and plant nutrients can all be assessed this way.

Rather than just tabling what nutrients are found in soils, as the Albrecht system does, the Reams soil test shows the bio-availability of these nutrients, using the Morgan extraction solution. This solution contains weak organic acids which mimic the acids released by the plant roots - their means of dissolving nutrients. [6]

In addition to providing an adequate supply of each nutrient, Reams also sought to determine a soil's proportional balance of:

- phosphorus to potash
- sulphur to nitrogen
- nitrogen to calcium
- calcium to magnesium and
- magnesium to potash and sodium.

Reams eventually established the following nutrient levels, in parts per million, for a minimally balanced, biologically active soil:

Calcium (Ca)	1000-2000 ppm
Magnesium (Mg)	145-285 ppm
Nitrate nitrogen (NO3)	20 ppm
Ammoniacal Nitrogen (NO3)	20 ppm
Phosphorus (P)	88 ppm
Potassium (K)	100 ppm
Sulphate (SO4)	100 ppm
Sodium (Na)	20-70 ppm
Conductivity	0.2-0.6 mS/cm
pH	6.2-6.8
ORP	130-260mV
Redox (rH)	25-28
Humus	<+ 3%
Paramagnetics	<+100cgs

Both testing systems are accurate for what they are showing, and obviously it would be ideal to do both tests on soil. But if this sounds too costly you might like to try the dowsers' methods of soil testing described later on in this book.

Minerals

A healthy soil requires an extensive range of trace elements to feed micro-organisms and sustain the humus complex, and the finer the particles these are supplied in, the quicker the microbes can incorporate them into it. Basalt rock dust is one of the best sources of minerals, having a wide range of trace elements.

Research has found much higher mineral content in organically produced, compared to conventionally produced, foods. Studies reported in the US Journal of Applied Nutrition showed that the average levels of essential minerals were much higher in organically produced apples, pears, potatoes and corn that were tested; while levels of mercury and aluminium were lower. An Australian study found higher levels of calcium and magnesium in organic foods. [6]

As well as nutrition - "Minerals are important to establish magnetic susceptibility characteristics, and humus is important in allowing the soil to utilise what it is now collecting. Both components are necessary for optimum soil fertility" says Anderson.

Minerals and health

Healthy soils produce healthy food which helps keep people healthy. This has been established over many decades by the organic growing movement.

Studies have shown what happens when we don't get enough minerals. For instance, a 1992 study of 72 Swedish communities, reported in the 'European Journal of Heart Disease', showed the result of drinking mineralised water. Cities with the highest level of minerals in water had the lowest incidence of heart disease. [7]

In the 1970's a study was made of the mineral status of criminals in a gaol in the USA. William J Walsh PhD found two distinct patterns emerge. The first was high copper to zinc ratio, low levels of sodium, potassium and manganese, and high levels of toxic lead and cadmium. These people experienced extreme mood swings, had poor responses to stress and occasional violent behaviour; although they did feel remorse for their wrongdoings. The second group was characterised by very low copper, very high sodium and potassium as well as high lead, iron and cadmium, plus low zinc levels. These people were often very violent and cruel, were pathological liars, fascinated by fire and had no remorse or conscience about their wrongdoings. [7]

The Centre for Disease Control says that one third of all Americans are chronically ill, yet 50 years ago it might have been 5 – 10% only. Soils have lost a lot a zing in those 50 years, since chemicals usurped natural fertilisers.

The 23 essential minerals for humans, listed in order of greatest to least amounts needed, are: nitrogen, phosphorus, potassium, calcium, magnesium, sulphur, iron, zinc, copper, manganese, boron, molybdenum, chlorine, sodium, cobalt, vanadium, silicon, iodine, selenium, chromium, lithium, nickel, arsenic.

Rock dusts are the cheapest and easiest sources of a range of minerals, but they must be carefully chosen. A mineral analysis is a good idea and each quarry should supply one.

A basalt dust tested by organic growers in northern NSW contained 0.4% phosphorus, 1.4% potassium, 9% calcium and 7.5% magnesium. To improve soil (depending on existing levels) one might wish to add calcium for an optimum balance of Ca:Mg, which is said to be between 3-7:1, depending on which school of thought is followed. [8]

Energy

Sunlight is the energy used to fuel the photosynthesis of plants. This is why seasons and daylength dictate what is planted and when. What is not so well known is that the sun also supplies a stream of magnetic energy which is also harnessed by plants.

The ancient Egyptians had a hieroglyph 'Ta Mari' which means that 'the Earth is the magnet of the sun' or 'Earth is the attractor of celestial energy'. [9]

Prof. Callahan was the first person in modern times to discover the significance of paramagnetism as a soil stimulant par excellence. He also discovered a third source of atmospheric energy that is utilised by the plant through its roots - weak light rays that are emitted by minerals.

Magnetism

Magnetism has many positive effects when applied to plant growth. Magnetic effects have now been well documented over the last couple of decades, with many pioneering studies done by Russian scientists, but before this time the concept had no official credibility, despite traditional and anecdotal evidence.

Plants exposed to magnetic fields have shown increased growth rates, increased production of sugars and oils, faster seed germination, etc. However this is not a general magnetic effect, it's only in relation to south pole magnetism, with its yang (stimulating) energy. When exposed to north pole (yin) energy - plant and animal growth is stunted and biological functions are reduced; however activity of the analytic thought mode (left brain hemisphere thinking) is enhanced.

Some people use magnets for polarising seed to enhance germination, and magnetised water for irrigation. Soviet scientists of the Volga Research Institute of Hydraulic Engineering and Land Reclamation reported that magnetised water can increase yields of tomatoes and cucumbers by up to 37%. Assistant director Dr Nikolai Yakovlev claims to have scientifically substantiated that magnetised water increases micro-biological activity of the soil, making it easier for plants to take up nutrients, thus increasing yields.

To test this for yourself it has been suggested that you need a strong horseshoe magnet, of about 1500 gauss, and a hose that will propel ordinary water between the magnet's two poles at a rate of one metre a second, or thereabouts, before it reaches the plant. On a small scale you can simply magnetise a jug of water, by placing the yang pole of the magnet uppermost beneath the jug and leaving it overnight, then watering pot plants with this magnetised water. I always test for the correct pole by dowsing.

Paramagnetism

Paramagnetism is defined as the weak attraction to a magnet. In soil it is a measure of the soil's ability to attract and hold energy. Paramagnetism is more subtle than ferromagnetism, which involves a significant presence of iron, nickel or cobalt.

"What is considered to occur within the paramagnetic material is that, when encountering an energy field, it alters the spin of it's molecules so that they are temporarily aligned with that field, i.e. they assume an increase in energy. This energy can then be transferred to the soil, plants and animals in the vicinity," explains Gary de Piazzi.

"The opposite force of paramagnetism is diamagnetism. This is when a non-magnetic material is repelled by a magnet, i.e. its molecules alter their spin so as to create an electrostatic field that is repulsed by a magnet."

Paramagnetic energy has been described as having an upward clockwise vortex, with diamagnetism having a downward anti-clockwise vortex. The dynamic interplay between paramagnetism and diamagnetism (- the harmonic dance of yin and yang) induces oscillating energy effects in the soil.

The source of the paramagnetic energy is the sun, says Callahan. The sun radiates magneto-electric dipoles, which are torn apart by sunflare activity into free magneto-electric monopoles of north (negative, yin) and south (positive, yang) polarity. These travel to Earth, where positive monopoles are absorbed and stored by paramagnetic stone, and soil, Irish Round Towers, etc.

The negative monopoles are adsorbed by plants, with some trickling out into the soil, to combine with the positive monopoles, and thus help stimulate plant growth.

The antenna capacity and magnetic susceptibility of paramagnetic rock is enhanced if rock has antenna shaped, sharp edged pieces, says Professor Callahan.

Callahan's Global Observations

Prof. Callahan determined in the 1980's that all fertile farm soils are both highly paramagnetic and diamagnetic . For instance the renowned grape growing region of South Australia at Coonwarra may have earned its reputation due to the presence of an underlying limestone (diamagnetic) belt, overlaid by paramagnetic basalt derived soil.

Callahan had deduced that ancient monumental mounds in Europe, known as dolmen, made from paramagnetic stone, actually affected agriculture by ordering the flux (Earth energy) lines which stimulate the seeds. It seems that paramagnetic materials, especially standing stones, stone circles and Irish Round Towers, have the ability to bend and focus the local magnetic field, as well as act as antennae for other biologically enhancing energies such as Schumann waves and extra-low-frequency radiowaves from the cosmos, he feels.

He noted that the Irish have long observed the tendency of their cattle and sheep to gather around such ancient stone structures.

Callahan had begun to notice that all of the politically agonised areas of the world, where wars and killing were commonplace, were the places where the Earth's magnetic field was not well conducted to the soil. Fascinated by this possible connection he began travelling around the world to test his hypothesis and ventured into the Amazon, an area still free from the effects of artificial electro-magnetic radiation, to investigate whether it was just human structures and unwise land management that resulted in low magnetic flow susceptibility in the soil.

He consistently found amiable and easy to live with natives in the river delta, where soil was deep and paramagnetic. Travelling upstream and upcountry, growth was still lush, although there was almost no topsoil, just a web of roots in the sparse dirt. There he detected only very poor magnetic penetration and low Earth magnetic flux intensity. This region was the home of very hostile headhunters!

Callahan's preliminary conclusion is that where magnetic fields cannot readily penetrate into the Earth, cultural breakup is the result. [10]

Callahan also finds a correlation between paramagnetic rock and sacred sites around the world. He was told by an Aboriginal man when visiting Australia that Uluru (Ayers Rock) was a special meeting ground, while a more important sacred site lay some 50 km (30 miles) away. He subsequently tested rock at both places. The Uluru rock was very low (only 30 or 40 cgs), whereas at the other sacred site it was very strong (at around 5000cgs).

People are also efficient antennae for collecting positive magneto-electric monopoles. A good ability to take in and release these charges signifies the 'magnetic healers' of the world, says Callahan.

The level of magnetic susceptibility of an area can give an indication of the temperament of the natives. The Irish battleground of Belfast sits on paramagnetic basalt, while laid-back Dublin has diamagnetic limestone beneath it. In Australia- Perth, on its flat sand and limestone coastal plain, is usually mellow and a bit sleepy; while Melbourne, located within a vast volcanic region, is known for it's lively cultural life.

Measuring paramagnetism

Getting to the technical details - paramagnetism is the ability of a non-magnetic material, when placed in the vicinity of a magnet, to be drawn towards that magnet. The degree of movement in one second is the magnitude of paramagnetism inherent that material. It is expressed in centimetres and grams per second (cgs).

" In a lot of cases this movement is extremely small e.g. aluminium has a reading of +16.5 (all of these figures are x10 -6), which translates to 1 gram of aluminium moving 0.0000165 centimetres towards a magnet in 1 second," explains Gary de Piazzi.

Generally a reading of 0-100 is considered poor, 100-300 is good, 300-700 is very good and 700-1200 is superior. Knowing the paramagnetic rate of soil and rock dust you can determine how much dust needs to be added.

The higher the cgs of a suitable rock dust, the less of it you will need to add to soil. When searching for suitable rock dust, most people would aim to find something with a minimum of 1000 cgs, depending on availability.

CGS Ratings with the PC Meter

Paramagnetic:

Oxygen	+3449cgs
Bunbury (WA) basalt	+650cgs
Lismore (NSW) basalt	+ 995cgs
Mt Gambier (SA) basalt	+4000cgs
Harkaway (Vic) basalt	+2000cgs

Diamagnetic:

Carbon dioxide	- 21cgs
Wanneroo (WA) limestone	- 20cgs
Bismuth	- 280cgs

Prof. Callahan measures Schumann waves in a tree.

The highest scoring basalt rock dust comes from the deepest and hottest magma. This spews out from the volcano and drops down, energised by oxygen, to the top of the volcanic cone and the high ground. The most highly paramagnetic rocks are always found on higher ground, with less energetic rock below.

This situation can become reversed. The paramagnetic force will erode over time, especially when rock is bare and exposed to the elements. Callahan has observed an exposed and weathered old granite mountain top that measured only 30 or 40 cgs. Around its base in a sheltered position the granite measured in at 2000 cgs.

Modern farming practices also speed up the erosion of forces, by eliminating minerals, organic matter and soil life, and replacing these with the quick fix of empty chemicals.

Inducing paramagnetism

Paramagnetism can make the difference between productive and dead soil, even when sufficient nutrient levels exist. So to impart paramagnetism will always enhance soil building processes and hence benefit the crops.

In the Blackbutt region of Queensland soils are reported to be extraordinarily high in paramagnetism, from 3000 to some 10,000 cgs. But it has been found that even soil with a 7000 cgs rating has been improved with the addition of rock dust of 2000 cgs.

Paramagnetism can be induced in soils merely by adding compost. A soil rated at 30 cgs was elevated to 70 cgs this way. And as American researcher Malcolm Beck observes "Paramagnetic rock and compost complement each other. They will work alone, but I have found each works much better when they are used together."

Paramagnetism has also been raised up to 700% by simply correcting the calcium/

magnesium ratio and increasing oxygen levels (e.g. by deep ripping the ground).

Paramagnetic stone circles and rock mulches around trees are also energetically beneficial, as are the Towers of Power, which act as paramagnetic antennaes, for enlivening the landscape.

Soil or rock that has been heated or burned will have elevated levels of paramagnetism, US researcher Malcolm Beck has found. Clay is paramagnetic and burnt clay even more so. No wonder, then, that plants in terracotta pots do better than in plastic pots.

Paramagnetic Oaks

All plants are diamagnetic, the polar opposite to the paramagnetic minerals. But there are exceptions. The oak is a classic example. It is a tree of many legendary associations.

Oaks were once held sacred to Thor/Taranis and the tree was assigned to Thursday, with Jupiter as it's ruling planet. Oaks were used as mark trees along county boundaries and were associated with lightning and the god Thor. They were said to be protective against it, because they 'courts the flash itself'. In fact lightning often strikes oaks, which are known to concentrate iron in their wood.

In the intriguing myth of Jason and the Argonauts a special piece of oak was used for the boat's prow. This was said to have oracular powers. The story is tied into the Sirius mystery and contains suggestions of ancient wisdom preserved as myth.

Until last century people married under special oak trees, such as one at Brampton, Cumbria, in a custom harking back to pagan times, when there were many 'marriage oaks', and also 'gospel oaks'. So it was a Christianisation of earlier times, when the sanctity of the sacred grove held sway. [11]

Oaks thrive in southern Australia and are a spectacular feature of central Victoria when resplendent in autumn colour.

Photo - Joy Finch

The Botanic Gardens in Melbourne, central Victoria and Adelaide have some excellent specimens of huge oak trees, many well over 100 years old. They are great places to discover natural resonance systems at work.

Stand under an oak and think about all that wonderful paramagnetic energy firing you up, as you breathe slowly and deeply. It's a great place for rest and revitalisation.

And psycho-spiritual processes may well be amplified within the tree's energy field (aura). You may then understand why humankind has always considered the oak perhaps the most sacred of the European trees.

Light from Rock

Callahan has found that paramagnetic rocks also emit light, at about 2000 to 4000 photons. If this rock is added to compost, the total emissions may rise to 400,000 photons. This is light for the plant roots to take up. "Plant roots are wave guides, just like insect antennae" says Callahan, an antennae expert.

Infra-red radiation

Callahan also says that plants emit infra-red rays which amplify scent molecules. Sick plants give off higher concentrations of the infra-red signals of ethanol and ammonia than healthy ones. Whereas healthy ones, grown on a good mineral soil, will radiate the infra-red microwave energies of the vitalising minerals.

Insects use their antennae to detect the source of scent molecules and can differentiate between healthy and unhealthy plants by their infra-red signatures. In this way insects are attracted to nutritionally deficient plants which are weak and ripe for attack. They are just doing their job of 'cleaning up the garbage'. [12]

Organic Matter

In an ideal soil, the level of organic matter is about 10% or more. The blacker the colour of the soil - the higher its organic matter level. The average organic matter content of farm soils is only around 3% these days.

The best source of organic matter is that which is grown in situ – the 'green manure' cover crop. Ideally this crop has the ability to fix nitrogen from the atmosphere. Clover and other members of the nitrogen-fixing legume family are ideal. Nitrogen is not given freely to soil though, for cover crops have to be slashed to release it and other nutrients from the corresponding amount of root matter that dies off below the surface. Legumes also need initial inoculation with mycorrhizal root bacteria, to maximise nitrogen-fixing ability.

Compost and mulch provide another favourite source of organic matter for microbes, the compost being already pre-digested.

Microbes

An extensive range of micro flora and fauna is a vital component of living soil. Chemical farming destroys beneficial micro-organisms and often increases the pathogenic ones. That's why the soil on many intensive farms could be considered dead.

Micro-organisms are the alchemists which transform the insoluble rock dusts into soluble minerals, ready for uptake by plant roots. They do this by producing weak digestive acid solutions which assist them in releasing ionic and colloidal mineral nutrients, vital to the soil's humus complex, and providing a major source of a plant's energy. Micro-organisms also aerate the soil, helping create a beneficial aerobic environment, high in paramagnetic oxygen, which is health promoting.

Microbial inoculants, even if only used in tiny trace quantities, can quickly increase microbe levels ten times, test studies have found. Compost is one form of inoculant, used since farming began. Provided it's well made, with a wide range of ingredients, it is an ideal way to add micro-organisms.

Compost will reduce the need for nitrogen applications and improves nitrogen efficiency, thanks to balanced nutrient levels. It also provides the food for microbes, who are able to fix large amounts of nitrogen from the atmosphere. Fish and seaweed sprays are also a good source of microbial inoculation.

Microbial stimulants are available in the market place, or you can always make your own. The biodynamic farmers have been using their biodynamic 'preps' successfully for decades, and these are a good form of inoculation too.

Nutritherm is a Victorian company which produce commercial microbial treatments. Their products are said to help create the healthy aerobic environment which knocks out most disease causing organisms, reducing the need for toxic sprays which harm the soil life. A golf course treated with Nutritherm microbes in Sydney has not had to spray for any pest problems in the 12 months since applying it, they report.

"You don't have to add microbial inoculants, although it does help", says Dr Arden Anderson. You probably won't need to if you spray out liquid fish, seaweed (best only on leaves), humic acid, compost, sugar or molasses. The molasses is good with liquid calcium, but not in high iron soils, and he recommends no more than ten litres (2 gallons) to one half hectare (one acre).

Kevin Heitman, a wheat farmer and water diviner from south east of Geraldton, W.A., has been experimenting with ways of improving his crops for the last 30 years, reported a local paper in 1999. He has had great success with simple microbial inoculants and also magnetism. He started off by magnetising the grain to see if it would grow faster. It did and the yield improved.

Later he selected soil which had experienced exceptional growth. He fermented this with fishmeal and flour and then sprayed the fermented mixture over the rest of the farm. There was a resulting boom in yield and quality. He now also magnetises the water he uses on crops as well. In 1998 he won WA's Top Crop Award for the biggest yield and the best grain.

17

Making Compost

The art of compost making derives from the observation that rich forest soils have a wealth of humus matter, derived from decaying mineral-rich leaves and diverse soil life, and these are kept constantly topped up by falling organic material. These soils are kept cool and moist by a surface layer of insulating mulch. Their colloidal humus particles retain water very well and also help keep micro-organisms and plants moist and fed.

We mimic the process in a compost heap and, if successful, create the very best soil amendment there is. Thin layers of alternating nitrogen rich and nitrogen poor layers of organic materials are spread over the heap, which is ideally at least a cubic metre (one cubic yard) in size when finished. Rich layers can comprise fresh lawn clippings, manure or kitchen scraps; while poor layers can consist of high carbon materials such as straw, weeds, dried grass etc.

The microbes that will decompose the materials prefer the ratio of carbon to nitrogen rich material to be between 25 - 30:1. So always make 'poor' layers thicker than 'rich' layers. (Horse stable sweepings would be around the right ratio, but beware that horses haven't just been wormed, or you will also kill your compost worms).

Between these layers sprinkle several kilos of paramagnetic rock dust and also some of the best topsoil you can find, to provide a ready source of micro-organisms. Comfrey and nettle leaves, and other herbs are a great addition too. Sprinkle some lime also if ingredients are too acid and smell sour.

Make sure everything gets thoroughly wetted as it goes onto the heap, to maintain an approximate 50% moisture level. Keep the heap damp as well as aerated. Place a cover of mulch, underfelt or carpet over the heap to protect it from the weather.

With a pitchfork turn the heap after a few weeks, when the heat generated has died down, to make sure all parts have been well composted down. If the heap was too dry to work properly, wet it down after mixing, recover and leave to try again. If it has been too wet and smelly, make a new heap with drier ingredients mixed into the smelly heap, and try again.

If you want to add compost worms – do this after the initial hot stage has finished, or they'll be cooked! After a couple of months compost should be ready for use. If it is still a bit hot then it will be very nutrient rich.

The best benefits from compost occur when it is simply spread on the top of topsoil. Earthworms will do the job of mixing it deeper. Always cover the compost layer with a protective layer of mulch, to stop nutrients eroding away or drying out.

Natural antibiotics present in compost means plant pathogens are greatly reduced when it is used and, when added to potting mixes, it greatly improves plant survival rates.

A good potting mix can be made for minimal cost by mixing compost (with any lumps removed) with coarse river sand and gravel at about 50:50. Into this can be added up to 10% of paramagnetic rock dust, for enhanced growth.

Never bury compost at the bottom of a tree hole. In fact if it is used deep down in subsoil it can give off hydrogen sulphide gas, which is toxic to plant roots. Don't place it too close to tree trunks or plant stems either, which might rot if choked by it.

A biodynamic compost heap.

A great microbial inoculant and fertiliser can be made by soaking compost or worm castings and diluting them at around 1:10 in water, then spraying this onto the soil. Some people have found this to be as effective as the biodynamic spray '500'.

Compost making is an exciting art of backyard alchemy. To think you have created a valuable microbial soil inoculant from waste products is nicely empowering. Each handful of well made compost is the home of several billion micro-organisms, who are all set to breathe added life into your farm or garden.

Traditional Japanese Inoculant

Douglas Graham has kindly passed on a recipe for a microbial soil inoculant which he says has been made by the farmers of Japan for thousands of years. It uses easily found materials that are specially fermented, then diluted and sprayed onto soil or plants.

<u>Bokushi</u> (pronounced Bok-ush-ee)
- Bran of any type – 10 litres (2 gallons)
- Oilseed meal of any type – 5 litres (1 gallon)
- Fish meal – 2.5 litres (1/2 gallon)
- Blood and bone – 2.5 litres (1/2 gallon)
- Your own best soil – 2.5 litres (1/2 gallon)
- Unchlorinated water – about 2 litres (1/2 gallon)
- Molasses – 20ml (1/10th pint)
- Well matured compost or worm castings – 20ml (1/10th pint).

In a 20 litre (4 gallon) container mix the dry ingredients thoroughly, then add water and molasses and mix thoroughly until the mixture is crumbly. Put this in a garbage bag and tie it up so that air is excluded as much as possible. Allow it to ferment for 5 – 7 days. It will have a sweet/sour smell when ready and can be used to make a soil activator called Ekihi. The mixture will keep for several months as long as air is kept out and it is kept in the shade.

Ekihi (pronounced Ek-a-hee)
This is the second stage in making the soil activator. Gather up:
- 200 litre (44 gallon drum)
- Water – approx 130 litres (30 gallon)
- Bokushi – 6.5 litres (1.5 gallon)
- Sea water - 6.5 litres (1.5 gallon)
- Molasses – 6.5 litres (1.5 gallon)
- Fresh grass clippings – 130 litres (30 gallon)
  preferably with dew on them.

In the drum build up layers of grass and Bokushi and when half way up pour in seawater and molasses. Then fill to the top with water and seal to keep air out. Leave for 3 days, and stir the mix each day for the next 5 – 7 days, until there are no more air bubbles, then drain off the liquid.

You can use the grass again 2 or 3 more times, just add the other ingredients again. Store the liquid in sealed containers, filling them right to the top, so air is not present.

To use Ekihi – mix one part of the liquid to 100 parts water. Experiment with different ratios to see which is best. Spray this onto the soil or plants in the evening, preferably after rain, as the microbes need moisture to multiply.

It's always best to only use Ekihi when you are feeling positive, as negative thoughts can hinder it's effectiveness.

Water

Water has a diamagnetic charge and is attracted to paramagnetic rock dust, which imparts excellent water retention capacity to soils. When water is influenced by paramagnetic rock dust it becomes 'restructured', that is - its molecules are re-aligned, which reduces surface tension significantly and enables it to be better absorbed by the plant. Water needs can be greatly reduced with this 'energised water', and on an ever drying continent this is good news for our over-stretched waterways.

Air

Compacted soil inhibits plant growth not only because roots and water find it more difficult to penetrate, but also because air is not present. Oxygen is a wonderful soil stimulant because it is highly paramagnetic, at about 4000 cgs. No wonder ancient cultures spoke of the pranic (energy) power of air and the benefits of breathing exercises (pranayama)!

Good soil structure, with plenty of worm burrows, allows air to circulate in soil. Micro-organisms and plants both absorb a great deal of carbon dioxide and, in tying up greenhouse gases, we can benefit the whole planet.

In the light of our energetic understanding of oxygen it is no wonder that hard, compacted soils have been greatly rejuvenated by a short term regime of deep ripping before cultivation begins. This alone has increased paramagnetic levels and soil fertility.

Eco-farming Strategies

In summary - the requirements of a fertile soil that's suited to growing nutrient rich food for us, can be met by making simple observations and low cost inputs of rock dusts, compost and mulch or cover crops.

If you don't want to bother with soil tests - that's fine! The micro-organisms in compost, some say, can transmute common elements to ones that are lacking - finding nature's own balance.

Remineralising your soil takes patience and good timing. Have the area deep ripped first off, as part of any initial earthworks undertaken. Permaculturists recommend a series of deep ripping treatments, to counteract compaction.

Check out soil for minerals status – volcanic loams are best, granite and clay soils can be good, but sandy soil will be low in minerals. The types of weeds present can indicate the fertility, acidity and mineral levels of the soil.

Experiment by broadcasting paramagnetic rock dust (several varieties if you can get it) at about 1 kg (2 lbs) to the square metre (one square yard) or 10 tonnes to the hectare (5 tons to the acre), and see what happens. Leave similar areas untreated as control plots for comparison.

For small areas spread some good compost thinly with the rock dust, and cover this over with a good layer of mulch. If soil is very acid - add a sprinkling of lime. For larger areas biodynamic or other microbial sprays and covercropping will complement the spreading of rock dust.

Autumn is the ideal time to apply rock dust to soils, allowing time over winter for soil making processes to work. Spread rock dust before or immediately after slashing the existing cover crop, and sow clover or another legume, with its complementary bacterial inoculant added.

The green manure crop will provide nitrogen and organic matter to complement the minerals.

Gradually the soil will come to life and be ready for planting in spring. Then you can stand back and watch the vegetative explosion!

References:

1 - Acres USA, 'Synthetics in Agriculture, Crow Miller, Nov 2000.

2 - 'PM Warned of Threat to River', M. Hogarth, Sydney Morning Herald, 14/12/98.

3 - 'Super Nutrition Farming', W. Peavey & W. Peary. Avery Publishing, USA, 1993.

4 - 'Living Downstream', Sandra Steingraber, USA.

5 - Gary de Piazzi supplied this information. He conducts the Reams soil analysis system through Bio-Test W.A. Pty Ltd. Ph. 08 9306 2643.

6 - Acres USA, 'Nutritional Quality: Organic Food versus Conventional', Mary Howell R Martens, Nov 2000.

7 - 'Remineralize the Earth', USA, autumn '98, no 12-13.

8 - 'Organic Info', Tweed-Richmond Organic Producers Organisation ,1995.

9 - 'Voices of the First Day – Awakening in the Aboriginal Dreamtime', Robert Lawlor, Inner Traditions, USA, 1991.

10 - Natural Resonance Study group newsletter, February 1999.

11 - 'Earth Harmony'. Nigel Pennick. Century Paperbacks, UK. 1987.

12 - 'Paramagnetism' by Phil Callahan, Acres USA, 1995.

2:2 *Rock Dust can Save our Soils*

Rock dust is a by-product of the quarrying industry, the fines which result from rock crushing. In the industry it is known as blue metal, cracker or crusher dust. Landscapers use rock dust for filling holes, bedding paving stones and mixing with cement. More recently its applications have broadened to other areas and its true importance is becoming apparent.

Over 100 years ago Julius Hensel wrote a book called 'Bread from Stones' which explained how crushed rock could improve soil fertility. His cause was taken up some nine decades later in the early 1980's by the late John Hamaker and Don Weaver. They asserted that impending climate change could be ameliorated by massive scale soil remineralisation, combined with reforestation, to provide a vegetative carbon dioxide sink. Their book 'Survival of Civilisation' was a landmark, while their warnings of climate instability have come true.

Demineralisation occurs rapidly on intensively farmed and tropical soils. Rockdust can reverse this process, restoring life to the soil by adding a myriad of minerals to feed micro-organisms and, given enough organic matter, helping to rebuild topsoil rapidly.

"Only with remineralisation," said John Hamaker "can the soil's micro-organisms obtain the nutrients they need to reproduce, lay down their bodies, and make the stable colloidal humus vital for plants, animals and humans to thrive on, as they once did before we demineralised the Earth."

Hamaker, whose book did more to promote soil remineralisation than any other single initiative, died in July 1994. He had previously been accidentally sprayed with toxic herbicide 24D, by a roadside spraying operation, and suffered debilitating illness from that time on.

In his last year of life he wrote to Barry Oldfield, president of the Western Australian Men of the Trees group, advocating the use of moraine gravels (from glaciers, absent in Australia) and urging the recognition that a healthy soil breeds up bacteria which can utilise all the atmospheric gases, including nitrogen and carbon dioxide, which then helps to stabilise climate change. [1]

A newsletter devoted to the benefits of rock dust was launched in 1986 in the US, and in 1994 this was upgraded into a quarterly magazine. 'Remineralize the Earth' was edited by Joanna Campe, but sadly, as of 2000, the magazine has ceased publication, partly because of the perception that this subject has finally become much more accepted by the mainstream, with many US universities and some government agriculture departments now doing their own research and taking action.

In the 1980's Phil Callahan brought our attention to the importance of paramagnetism to plant growth and showed how volcanic rock dusts can supply this energy to soils. Many people regard his claims as far fetched, but such is the fate of all new ideas.

Callahan & students in Australia, Aug '93.

Trials

In Australia the benefits of rock dust have been scientifically documented since 1997 by the Australian construction company Boral, which owns over 200 quarries.

The Boral scientists have taken a holistic approach, studying the effects of applying rock dusts to potting mix alone, and in combination with 'sweetpit'(a limestone based, diamagnetic soil preparation) and artificial fertilisers in varying amounts. The best impact on plant growth was when all three were applied together.

Trials have shown that rock dust improves soil pH, water retention capacity, microbial activity, root to shoot ratio, plant health generally, seed germination rates and the humus complex, while it increases plant height and weight and reduces plant mortality. Rock dust makes a good replacement for sand in growing media, they found. Boral is now recognised as a world leader in scientific research into rock dusts as soil improvers.

During Boral's many plant trials there was inexplicable lush growth of control plants. These were growing in close proximity to the rock dust treated plants. It became apparent to researchers that a purely paramagnetic affect was at work here. It was verified by pot trials by the Men of the Trees group in Western Australia. One MOTT trial involved burying little plastic bags of rock dust in the plant pot. Amazingly - this was enough to enhance plant growth, despite no physical contact between plant roots and rock dust.

Cost effectiveness

Good farming techniques, with the application of added rock dust and sufficient organic matter, will enhance the paramagnetic and diamagnetic intensity of the soil. With a good level of microbial activity, this builds great soil structure with a colloidal humus complex. The benefit to farmers is not only cost effective, in comparison with the cost of chemical fertilizers, but environmentally enhancing.

A careful cost-benefit analysis of using the commercial basalt dust mixture Min-Plus at the Harding Brothers banana plantation in Queensland has seen trials running since 1985. Overall outcomes saw fertiliser applications reduced by 80%, dolomite applications down by 50%, whilst magnesium deficiency, a previous problem, was not detected after 16 months.

The bananas became healthier, growing 20% faster than usual and producing a 25% better yield. The total of cost savings plus increased yield equated to an $AUD56,722 per hectare ($25,500 per acre) benefit. [2] Adding to that the reduced environmental impact of less chemical run-off and it has been win-win all round.

Paramagnetic products

Fertiliser companies such as Alroc and Nutri-Tech Solutions are helping to promote the many benefits of rock dust through the marketing of their paramagnetic rock dust based products. NTS reports an American study that recorded a threefold increase in microbial activity from the use of relatively small additions of paramagnetic materials.

Alroc supplies various mixtures, in granulated form- such as basalt/ granite/ dolomite/ calcium bentonite; basalt/ granite/ lime /bentonite; the first mix plus coal fines for carbon or with rock phosphate; and a mixture with added superphosphate and artificial fertilisers. Some of their blends also have extra boron, zinc, copper and molybdenum added. (However it is recommended to first establish specific soil needs before buying such formula mixes.)

Boral made an extensive literature search on the subject and found a list of paramagnetic intensities for various rocks types. The highest reading, being rock from Kings Canyon, had a rating of 4,795cgs. Their own testing has found what must be some of the highest rated rock in the world, with the basalt from their Kiama quarry ranging between 4,830 – 6090cgs. Boral is marketing a mix of its best rock dusts as 'Nu-Soil', as well as a product called 'sweetpit', which has been developed for the Japanese market. Sweetpit is derived from selected limestones and sugars, so it's a source of diamagnetic minerals.

Granite

Different rock dusts are suited to different crops. While the rock dust of choice is any highly paramagnetic basalt (with low iron level), in Western Australia granite is more easily available. As early as 1991 the Men of the Trees showed that granite dust added to potting mix could stimulate the healthy growth of seedlings at their nursery, Amery Acres.

A MOTT trial saw a fivefold increase in growth for some seedling eucalypts and shortened potting out time from five months to six weeks when one particular granite dust was added to potting mix. However the same granite dust was used on a wheat crop which experienced total failure – it was a headless crop! (Nearby, biodynamic wheat farmer Malcolm Borgward went on to harvest a fabulous wheat crop, at 10 tonnes to the hectare, thanks to the addition of diorite rock dust, which he had selected by kinesiology.)

Masters student Cathy Coroneus in trials with the Men of the Trees showed, in 1994, that granite rock dust would release potassium to plants and also retain it from leaching, which sandy soils plus potassium chloride could not do. She also observed that with as little as 0.05% granite dust added to a non-wetting soil, the water infiltration time could be halved. Curtin University and MOTT have studied granite dusts as potential soil enhancers but not had very good results. Hugh Lovel has written that granite and gneiss dusts in the US contain over 25% silicon, with 4% potassium and 0.5% to 0.7% phosphorus, as well as various trace elements. [1]

Granite and the ancients

Granite is known to be radioactive in some degree and associated with radon gas emissions. People once considered small doses of radon to have healing effects, and would bathe in the radon rich airs of caves. Areas where high levels of radon are found do not necessarily present the expected high lung cancer rates, studies have shown. Sometimes a reverse scenario is found, with less cancers occurring. The healing spring waters of Bath and the Chalice Well in the UK are known to be radioactive.

The Egyptians referred to granite as maat, the stone of spirit, and the King's Chamber in the Great Pyramid is lined with it. This chamber, along with a multitude of prehistoric granite monuments around western Europe, has high radon gas levels. The Dragon Project, studying English stone circles of antiquity, found granite stone circles to have very active spots which emit constant streams of gamma radiation.

The Project's Paul Deveraux surmises that granite may have been the stone of choice because its energies had psycho-spiritual effects on people. It is thought that the elevated levels of radiation and the ionised air of sacred caves and around paramagnetic and radioactive stone circles could have affected brain hormone levels and helped people attain altered states of consciousness during ceremonial rituals. Serotonin brain hormone levels would have been affected, as well as beta-carbolines, which are thought to enhance dream imagery and visions. [3]

Will any dust do?

If soil hasn't the right nutrient mix to match the crop, then using any old rock dust may not help, and could even prove toxic to some degree.

While basalt rock dust is a major source of trace elements it lacks the essential macronutrients nitrogen, phosphorus and, to a lesser extent, potassium. Boral suggests blending different types of rock dust, such as granites and river gravel, plus added minerals, to make up for any deficiency. [4] While commercial enterprises do various rock dust mixes to broaden the spectrum of minerals, this still may not suit your soil's individual requirements.

High iron levels can be a problem in some soils (which are often a red colour), so a poorly selected basalt rock dust or lava scoria might add excess iron if not applied in careful measure. Iron is needed for photosynthesis, but too much can combine with aluminium to lock up phosphate and trace elements in acid soil types. 10 - 50 parts per million of iron in fertile soils is considered sufficient.

Effects of using rock dusts

* Increased yields

In scientific studies soil remineralisation with rock dust has been shown to increase yields by between two to four times in agriculture and forestry (with increased wood volumes). [5]

* Lower mortality

People report lower mortality rates in crops which have been treated with rock dust. In the Boral plant trials during a 44 °C (115 °F) heatwave there was an instance of a vent not being opened to cool down the glasshouse. Many plants were 'fried' brown in the heat and looked like they were finished. But 48 hours later the ones with added rock dust and sweetpit were rejuvenated and looked healthy again, whereas all the others were well and truly dead.

*Pest suppression

People report less pest control is required after soils are improved with rock dusts and plants have become vibrantly healthy. In trials run by the Men of the Trees in Perth, seedlings grown in granite dust enriched potting mix did not get nibbled by caterpillars, as did the controls. [1]

One of the Boral trials looked at the effect of rock dust on nematodes, a plant pest in soils. Rock dust was applied to a major sporting ground that suffered turf nematodes and it did prove effective. A plant pathologist was then employed to further study this effect in a scientifically replicable trial. The results showed that plants in biologically active soil with high levels of rock dust could maintain vigorous growth, despite the presence of the nematodes, which would normally have damaging effects. Tomatoes grown in these trials were 21% taller than the controls, with a 65% greater dry weight..

Relevant studies show increased pest resistance from organic as compared to conventionally produced crops. A study by Dr Franco Weibel at the Research Institute of Organic Agriculture in Ackerstrasse, Switzerland found that organically produced apples had higher phenol levels. Phenols are naturally synthesized by plants as a defence against pests and diseases. [6]

Research in Germany has found that very fine rock dust sprayed directly on plants will deter insects. Also – trails of rock dust around plants can be a good physical barrier against snails and slugs.

* Fungal protection

The aerobic conditions fostered by rock dusts and microbes are not favourable for fungal activity. Georg Abermann, an Austrian agricultural consultant and forester, finds that silicium and other fresh trace elements improve resistance to fungal attack. Silica is well supplied by granite and other rock dusts, while the anti-fungal biodynamic preparation 501 is basically silica, made from crushed rock crystal.

Many people around the world have enjoyed fungal free crops thanks to rock dust. Using it in potting mixes with compost reduces the 'damping off' of seedlings from fungal attack, as well as generally suppressing pathogens.

* Weed suppression

Some people report a suppression of weeds. Whether this is from the physical barrier of a layer of rock dust around trees, or a change in the soil status that does not foster weeds, remains to be studied. Other people report lush weed growth in the enhanced growing conditions.

Darryl uses pink granite rock dust as a mulch for quandong trees at 'Felchillo Oasis', Streaky Bay, S.A.

* Improved Flavour

Abermann also finds that rock dust improves the aroma and taste of the harvest. This I can vouch for, and other peoples' anecdotal evidence agrees. Trace elements allow the formation of aroma enzymes in plants. Mineralised hay has a stronger aroma, which animals then eat with all the more gusto, he says.

* Improved Quality

With produce from rock dusted soil there is a general enhancement of quality. There is no one standard test for quality, but improved nutritional levels are a good indication, as are the presence of large complex molecules such as sugars, proteins, enzymes, esters and organic acids.

It is now proven that organically produced foods have elevated nutritional levels. Boral is monitoring the oleic fatty acid content of olive oil, at its olive plantation field trials, as a measure of quality.

* Brix

Mineralised soils produce crops with increased Brix readings, due to higher sugar levels. The Brix index reading is done with a refractometer, in a technique developed by Dr Carey Reams in the early 1980's. Plants grown in paramagnetic soils tend to have a visible blue tinge, due to increased sugar levels, which equates to better flavour, pest and frost resistance and health of plants. Some researchers report a 6 point Brix increase with crops grown in paramagnetic soils.

* Human health

Callahan used principles of paramagnetism to cure himself and his son of illness. They ate a tablespoon of fine rock dust and a teaspoon of garlic daily, and wore special vests soaked in seawater, to amplify ELF waves. Now Callahan's lung cancer is gone and his son's arthritis also.

Schindele in Austria markets his finely ground rock dust throughout Europe as a mineral dietary supplement. He has changed his hair colour from grey back to its original brown, by eating some daily. [7]

Many people have successfully experimented with gaining the benefits of rockdust directly, by taking a teaspoonful of fine basalt dust in a glass of water daily. They simply stir it up, drink the cloudy water and leave the grits in the bottom. (If you regularly down the lumps you can end up with colon problems, it has been found.)

* As pH enhancement

Acidity in soils, whether natural or induced by chemical farming, tends to lock away nutrients, such as calcium and phosphates, from plants. Superphosphate is very acidifying, with triple super the worse type and mono super the least bad form. (It's better still to supply slow release phosphate in the form of untreated rock phosphate that has been composted.) Rock dust is a great additive to acid soils, as it can help increase soil pH (thus reducing acidity).

Aluminium is also released when soils are acid and if this gets into our systems, free radical damage can occur in our tissues. Aluminium toxicity is also linked to repetitive strain injury and Alzheimers disease, which are far more prevalent since aluminium cooking pans became popular after the war.

Most people apply lime to increase soil pH, but this can cause problems in itself. Biodynamics researcher and student of Steiner Ehrenfried Pfeiffer warned that the use of lime can 'burn out' the humus complex, as it overstimulates soil and plant processes.

This was seen in Austrian trials which compared rock dust and lime added to soil and the subsequent changes in soil pH over 87 days. Within 24 hours the soil that had been limed had risen from a low pH 4 to an optimum of pH 7. Such a huge increase in the ion count is very stressful to plants. The pH scale is logarithmic, going from 1 to 14, the scale being actually 10 to 10^{14}. Such a sharp pH rise meant an increased ion count from 100,000 to 100,000,000 ions! Plants can become sick with the shock of this rate of change.

After the 87 days the rock dusted soil also ended up with a pH of 7, but it was a very gradual rise spread over the time, which did not incur any plant stress at all. [4]

* Easier cultivation

Improved soil structure makes life easier all round. Abermann reports that during spells of wet weather, soils now do not get boggy since using his company's Bio-Lit rock dust in the interrow spaces of vineyards. Good soil aeration has taken place and it is possible to travel with mechanical equipment between vines without the usual compaction of the sub-surface soil. Less cultivation is also required for the interrow cover crops to thrive.

* Frost resistance

Many growers have found that increased sugar levels in plants acts as anti-freeze. Aberman, for instance, reports that frost resistance of grape vines was significantly increased after the application of Bio-Lit rock dust and subsequent formation of a good humus complex.

* Reduced soil salinity

In Western Australia salt deserts are taking over good agricultural land at a rate of 100,000 hectares (220,000 acres per year). These soils are some of the oldest in the world and agriculture is highly perilous there. But rock dust and microbes plus revegetation can turn it all around, trials are showing.

According to author David Hall the paramagnetic values of the rock dust product Eco-Min "seems to separate the sodium from the chlorine, allowing chlorine to break down in sunlight in saline soils." [8]

Nutritherm reports that salt levels have dropped from 2500 EC units to about 500 ECs at an Adelaide golf course in the 12 months since applying Nutritherm microbes to turf. It seems that by enhancing biological activity in soils, we can foster a natural reduction in soil salinity. This has been also shown by Canadian research, now being emulated in WA. [9]

The Men of the Trees are conducting a trial where they are reafforesting a salt pan at Nambling. They have spread woodchips as a mulch around most of the trees and the mulched ones have enjoyed 100% survival.

"This is in line with research by Dr Giles Lemur of Quebec University, who states that the best way to regenerate salt affected soils is to mimic forest litter, with tree prunings no bigger than 7cm. These must not be spread too thick, to allow the sun to penetrate the soil. This recipe encourages the growth of mycorrhizal fungi, which feed minerals to the trees and the trees return the favour by giving the fungi sugar." [9] If rock dust and molasses or sweeptpit had been spread as well in this trial - one would assume an even better result.

The revegetation of large areas (especially higher ground) and use of salt tolerant plants, such as the fodder plant saltbush, effects a lowering of the water table and thus reduces surface salinity. This is particularly effective if plantings are over recharge zones, which can be found by dowsing (water divining). Dowser David Kennett of WA suggests planting trees (selected by dowsing) directly over underground streams.

With what is already known - why wait for more scientific investigation here? We can combat dryland salinity with the ecological approach of revegetating landscapes using permaculture farm planning principles and dowsing, and by rehabilitating the soil with rock dust, microbial innoculants and organic matter.

* Going organic

Chemically farmed land was cleaned up by a product which contains paramagnetic rock dust combined with microbes, reported Joanna Campe. One year later tests found there were no signs of chemicals in the soils. So this technique can be used to speed up the transition time needed to be certified as an organic grower. [5]

* Shelf life

Produce grown on mineral rich soil will have a longer shelf life, as its more vital integrity resists rotting better.

* Forestry

Abermann observed the accidental benefits of rock dust that had blown over dying Austrian forests during road construction. The forests came back to life and tests were subsequently done which successfully duplicated this effect.

Even if it's only a single application, plantation forestry can greatly benefit by the spreading of rock dusts over sites, it has been found. In long term experiments by the timber industry in one central European forest large quantities of basalt dust were applied to the pine forest soils. Over a 24 year period four times the usual volume of wood was achieved. One single application plot outperformed the control for an amazing 60 years. [5]

* Odour reduction in manure

Boral has done successful trials on odour reduction in animal manures and sewage sludge and is well on the way to marketing a soil improver combining rock dust and sludge. The rock dust had a pronounced reductive effect on odorant chemical emissions, and thus odour, in the first 24 hours after treatment. There was a partial recovery of odours a few days later. Composting processes were also accelerated with added rock dust.

Abermann's company Sanvita in Austria has been conducting trials with their Bio-Lit rock dust along these lines also. When they added it to dung in animal pens at 20 – 30 kg per cubic metre (44 - 66 lbs/cubic yard) of solid or liquid waste, or added it to composting dung at 2% of mass, they found reduced odours and accelerated composting processes. [10]

* Feeding rock dust to animals

Abermann says that when 2% Bio-Lit was added to fodder, the protein levels in cows' milk were increased by 0.3%. When 2% Bio-Lit was added to pig and poultry feed there was a reduced incidence of diarrhoea and better fodder utilisation.

To explain these effects Abermann surmises that finely ground rock dust creates very favourable and stable life conditions for the micro-flora in the stomach and guts of the animals, as well as in the compost heaps and soil profile, leading to higher multiplication rates of the microbes. Harmful anaerobic micro-flora don't have a chance.

Spreading rock dust on pastures for dairy cows is another successful means of imparting minerals. Abermann say pastures grow lushly, milk production goes up and calving mortality drops. His Bio-Lit rock dust, which is 51% silica, is bulk delivered in 26 tonne tanker trucks directly to the slurry tanks on farms. Mixed with the effluent, this is then put onto pastures at a rate of 800kg rock dust to the hectare (1.7 ton to the acre) per year and the cows prefer this pasture to any untreated pasture.

* Healing rocks

In many ancient cultures around the world rocks have been used to facilitate healing processes. This tradition is resurfacing, with basalt rocks now being used as adjuncts to new age therapies. Vogue Beauty 2000 (UK) describes 'La Stone' therapy, which involves placing basalt stones on chakra (people's energy centre) points. [11]

* Combatting blue-green algae

Several people have reported that basalt rock dust added to waterways poisoned by blue-green algae can successfully combat outbreaks.

* Anti-termites

It has been found that rock dust can make a good physical barrier against marauding termites, when spread under houses in a 100mm (4") thick layer. 'Granite-Guard' is a commercial product based on this principle. Much better than spraying toxic chemicals under the house at regular intervals, with people breathing the emitted fumes for ever more. However some find it not as effective as anticipated.

* Anti-radiation

High levels of paramagnetism are able to counteract electromagnetic radiation and radioactivity, it is beginning to be found. People can eat some types of rock dust to flush radioactive particles from their body. (The victims of nuclear war at Hiroshima survived better than expected thanks to their diet of mineral rich foods such as seaweeds and miso.) Rock dust is being used in the manufacture of an ever growing range of commercial personal protection devices and experimental environmental EMR stress reduction installations (see next chapter).

* Improving rainwater

Rainwater is fairly neutral and mineral free, but it can pick up acids, metals and salts from the air and rooftops. You can neutralise this acidity and improve mineral content by dangling a giant 'tea bag' of paramagnetic rock dust in the rain tank and jiggling it occasionally.

* Restructuring water

Water is highly responsive to its environment and is easily contaminated. When in contact with paramagnetic rock dust water will have its molecular structure rearranged and consequently surface tension is reduced. It is then more readily taken up by soil and plants and is in a more beneficial form, enhancing plant and animal health and growth.

"There is also better taste, reduced chlorine smells, reduced scale in fittings and pipes, better cleaning properties and better hydration in the body, and other benefits" writes Tim Strachan, who makes 'Energised Water Systems' for The Energy Store, Sydney. [12]

Commercial water energiser systems combine small quantities of rock dust and other substances in two half shells or sleeves which are attached around the incoming water supply pipes.

The concept is based on the global observation that people gain benefit from healing springs which are associated with paramagnetic basalt rock. The producer of the Water Activator states that it is "made from basalt and other particles in a particular form that replicate the magnetic effect causing the formation of concentrations of complex water clusters, which characterise living, vital water. The water energy is 'entrained' to reach higher levels of resonance. In the process the molecular structure of the water transfers from the energy depleting left hand spin to the energising, vitalising right hand spin."

The Water Activator, like other models, creates 'restructured' water which is then better equipped to carry out functions in the body, such as flushing out toxins. The water feels softer, lathers better, has reduced lime scaling and corrosion effects on pipes etc, chlorine odours are reduced, while it is very beneficial for plants too. The quality of grey water is also improved with the activated water of higher resonance." [11] Water energiser systems are becoming very popular in spa resorts, where hydrotherapy demands the best quality water.

However, to balance the claims, it has been communicated to me by Boral that one rock dust based water energiser product has been tested by their team and the treated water was found to have no stimulant effects on plant growth at all.

As there are no governments standards in relation to such new products - it is a case of 'buyer beware'. See if you can trial a system first before you buy it and check it out for yourself.

* Grey Water Systems

In relation to waste water treatment, quality of grey water is also improved when water energiser systems are used, say manufacturers.

It has also been observed that grey water reed ponds, designed to help cleanse water naturally by the action of water reeds, function best when basalt, as opposed to other types of gravel, is used to fill them. [13]

Sources of rock dust

Basalt quarries are the best sources of paramagnetic rock dust. You will find quarries listed in the yellow pages of your phone book. Landscaping shops are the next best place to find rock dusts. Be aware that within each rock deposit there will be material with differing degrees of paramagnetism.

Black area show extensive volcanic activity in eastern Australia.

Granites may or may not be paramagnetic. Victorian samples I have tested have not been paramagnetic, while the mainly pink granites of South Australia and south west WA are very good (although less than 1000 cgs). Pink granite with black inclusions is said to be best.

Many good basalt sources are found in Victoria, where volcanic activity was once widespread in central and western districts. The Harkaway quarry basalt, east of Melbourne, rates at about 2000cgs.

To the north there's quarries at Violet Town; in central Victoria there's the Waterfall Quarry at Carisbrooke, near Maryborough; in western districts here are several, including quarries near Moree, Stawell and Harrow - with no doubt many others well worth checking out.

Just over the border in South Australia there is the sought after basalt at Mt Schank, south of Mt Gambier (4000cgs); while Streaky Bay on the west coast of Eyre Peninsula has beautiful pink granite (that was used to face the new Parliament House in Canberra) of around 300cgs.

Near Canberra there is a basalt quarry at Jugiong, while around Sydney there's Peats Ridge and Prospect, and the very best rock at Boral's Bombo quarry, south of Sydney, near Kiama (- to contact the Nu-Soil people for details, phone Tony Zdrilic 02 9688 9903).

There are several basalt quarries in northern NSW, including the Lismore Council quarry (995cgs) and one (of two) at Teven, at 3,400cgs.

In the huge state of WA there are only relatively small areas of basalt in the south western corner, with some beautiful outcrops along the coastline. Bunbury basalt quarry, south of Perth, has rock at 650cgs, while there's excellent basalt at Manjimup (around 6000cgs). There's some good gabbro rock in the north and pink granite north of Albany in the Porongorups, a mountain range and national park.

In Tasmania there's some strongly paramagnetic rock at Devonport. In Queensland Mareeba quarry fines tested at 1600cgs, while scoria at Mount Quinkan, near Lake Eacham on the Atherton Tablelands was quite good, but iron content was very high, although I'm told it grows great orchids.

A tree grows out from solid pink granite, Porongorups, s-w WA.

Basalt outcrop, Fingal, nth NSW.

It is ideal to use natural basalt rocks from your own land for stone circles in the garden. But don't over-harvest, as rocks provide important shelters for small creatures and are part of the ecology of the landscape. And be aware that 'wild harvesting' of rock on public land may well be illegal, without first obtaining a special license.

If you want to check out your local quarry's produce, it's a good idea to get a copy of the mineral analysis from them, and check for high levels of iron, which will give false readings when testing for paramagnetism and other unwanted affects.

You can gain an idea of the level of paramagnetism by slowly waving a magnet under a sheet of paper over which you have sprinkled a little rock dust. If the particles move towards and with the magnet, and are attracted more than other samples, there will be a useful degree of paramagnetism.

Application rates & regimes

At most quarries I've visited I have been allowed to fill a few bags with rock dust free of charge - enough for a household vegetable garden. If you buy tonnages you might have to pay around $15 per tonne - still inexpensive. The big cost is in transportation. Get together with friends and neighbours and share a truckload for best economy.

Optimum application rates recommended by Boral research are 5 – 10 tonnes per hectare (2-4 tons to the acre). Above the maximum rate and there is a levelling off of affects, so it's not worth overdoing it. Because the cost of transport and spreading of rock dust on the broadacre is not cheap, it is recommended to put more out at less frequent intervals to reduce such costs. That is, instead of spreading 5 tonnes to the hectare every 2 or 3 years, it is more economical to spread 10 tonnes/ha every 5 or so years. However smaller amounts, even as little as a 1-2 tonnes/ha (a half to one ton to the acre) will bring good results, when applied more often. [4]

Austrian farmers have found it beneficial to spread rock dust around the time of slashing the cover crop. They observe that the more aerobic environment created on the soil surface helps the 'green manure' crop to rot down more easily.

If seeking only the paramagnetic values of rock to impart to soil, you can add it in chip form for a one-off application. Chips are cheaper to produce and will not erode away like the finer dust. By choosing material with higher paramagnetic values you can reduce

Fabulous paramagnetic pink granite boulders at Streaky Bay, west coast Eyre Peninsula, South Australia.

quantities needed, making substantial savings on expensive transportation. If you obtain the usual finest screenings of 5mm (one quarter inch) dust you will have a range of particle sizes from powdery dust to small sharp pieces that give the paramagnetic antenna affect as advocated by Prof. Callahan.

A Warning

So much for the good news about using rock dusts – there has to be a downside! And so here's a word of warning. The fine particles are a hazard if breathed in, as the silicaeous dusts can be as dangerous as asbestos to the lungs.

So it is advisable to always wear dust masks whenever this could be a hazard. And cover your load or wet it down during transport or it may blow away!

Testing the theory

You can test all the theories out for yourself on a small scale, and this can be a good way to gauge the effectiveness of selected inputs. For the purely energetic effect place pieces of paramagnetic stone in a number of plant pots mixed with soil, and have some control pots without rock at several metres (yards) distance. Compare the growth of, say, radish seedlings or wheat sprouts.

Plants ideally prefer to get their rock dust after it has been incorporated into compost. Hugh Lovel recommends no more than 10% of the finest rock dust be added to compost heaps.

In the backyard, try using about one kilo of rock dust per square metre (2 lbs to the square yard) of garden plot, plus some compost, mixed into the top few inches of topsoil, then mulch it and keep it moist. Leave areas that have not been treated to act as control plots. Then sow seeds or plant out and compare the results.

References -

1 - Men of the Trees (WA) Report no 7, March 1995.
2 - Acres USA, 'Remineralising our Soils' Joanna Campe, April 1995.
3 - 'Symbolic Landscapes', Paul Deveraux, Gothic Image, 1992.
4 - 'Soil Remineralisation with Basaltic Rock Dust in Australia'
      I Dumitru, A Zdrilic, A Azzopardi, Boral Construction Materials, Sydney, 1999.
5 - 'Remineralize the Earth' issue 12-13.
6 - 'Nutritional Quality: Organic Food versus Conventional', Mary-Howell R Martens,
      Nov. 2000, Acres USA, PO Box 91299, Austin, Texas, 78709, USA.
7 - 'Secrets of the Soil' C. Bird and P. Tompkins, Harper and Row,1989.
8 - 'Soils or Spoils' vol. 2, David Hall, 18 Jarvis Place, Arundel, Qld 4214, Australia.
9 - Natural Resonance Group newsletter, Nov. 2000.
10 - Georg Abermann, 1997, Sanvita Pty Ltd, Oberndorf, Austria.
11 - 'Spa Australasia' magazine, 2000, vol.5.
12 - The Energy Store, Sydney, email : strachan@megadisc.com.au
13 - Personal communication from Tony Kolenberg,
      Lismore N.S.W. City Council health/building inspector, 2000.

The Benefits
of
'Stone Age Eco-Farming'

To summarise the benefits of 'stone age farming', where increased levels of minerals, organic matter and microbes are incorporated into soils:

Enhancement of soil in respect of:

soil structure
humus complex,
microbial activity,
water retention capacity,
improved drainage
faster conversion to organically certified production
easier cultivation
accelerated composting processes
odour reduction when composting manures

In relation to plant growth and harvest, an increase of:

plant height and weight,
root to shoot ratio
seed germination rates,
plant health
sugar levels (Brix)
crop quality, quantity, nutritional values and flavour
health of livestock and people
farm profitability and sustainability.

For plants and soil - overall reductions in respect of:

plant mortality
soil acidity
frost damage
pest damage
fungal problems
need for chemical sprays and chemical run-off
tendency to soil erosion
need for irrigation
soil compaction
production costs
soil salinity.

2:3 Restoring Natural Resonance

We have all contemplated the depressing scenario of nuclear waste from accident or war poisoning vast areas with devastating long term effects. That rocks could radiate an unhealthy energy, in the form of ionising radiation is a plain fact. As uranium is a commercial commodity it has been intensely studied for its economic potentials.

It is now gradually being recognised that other rocks have the opposite capacity - they resonate with beneficial energies, such as paramagnetism, and their energy fields can actually counteract radioactivity and other harmful energies.

Christopher Bird gives an example of our newfound understandings in that marvellous book 'Secrets of the Soil'. He writes that Azomite, a form of montmorillonite rock, is being mined for its health giving trace elements in the USA. A great advocate of this rock dust is veterinary doctor C. S. Hansen who attributes its amazing properties to the idea that trace elements radiate microwaves. He feels that it is this microwave radiation in the plants which is detected by the insects via their antennae, and that the lack of any mineral radiation signals to the insects to come over and 'clean up the garbage'.

Hansen explained to Bird that, when spread around crops that were laden with pesticides, herbicides and heavy metals, the effects of these toxins were neutralised throughout the plant within four minutes by the presence of azomite. He explained that this affect was due to radiations from the trace elements catalysing the toxins into harmless compounds that the plant can use or return to the soil.

Callahan discovered that as well as insects and bacteria, chemical elements also radiate electro-magnetic signals to find, recognise and join each other.

This confirmed clairvoyant understandings, such as the drawings by Theosophists Leadbeater and Besant, which showed elements covered in horns, spikes and antlers, for energy reception and communication. Rudolph Steiner (see chapter 3.1) had also long ago hinted at this when he mysteriously stated that "the elements are sentient". [1]

Protection from radiation

An Austrian called Schindele discovered the benefits of rock dust applied to the dying forests of Austria. He revived not only his trees with it but also turned his hair back from grey to brown, after taking two spoonfuls daily. The product is now marketed throughout Europe as a mineral dietary supplement.

Tests by the University of Vienna found that Schindele's rock dust could even work against radioactivity and this was confirmed by a Soviet Institute for atomic physics in the Ukraine. Under the micropolariscope it was revealed that the rock dust had an altered molecular and atomic lattice and that this produced effects on ionized radioactive particles in the body. [1]

Another Austrian, the late Dr Gernot Graefe, born 1937, started to investigate the energetic effects of rock dusts around 1982. Graefe was a renowned soil and humus specialist, working for the Austrian Academy of Science. When he read Hamaker's book he realised that minerals were the missing link in soil research. He was soon applying rock dusts with composted grape remains to dying forests and bringing them back to life, with the well researched belief that 'soil is the basis for our present and future existence.'

Graefe decided that the Earth's thin layer of topsoil 'represents a level for exchange and buffering of the climate which is more important for the ecological balance than is yet acknowledged.' Fierce winds and thunderstorms will be weakened when there are improved interactions between topsoils and the atmosphere, he believed.

In 1987 Graefe started his bioenergetic research and found that liquid extracts from organically grown grapes could 'interfere with the effects of gamma radiation in tissues'. More investigation found good effects with other forms of electro-magnetic radiation. Humus, it seems, has evolved to filter and transform environmental energies. In colleague Dr Felsenreich's words- 'every well adjusted humus cover purchases all incoming vibrational energies'.

In Graefe's view the cause of the death of the forests in Europe is fourfold: it stems from increased background atomic radiation, from nuclear testing and accidents; increased radiation from tele-communications; increased roentgen radiation from the sun, due to the thinning of the ozone layer; and fourthly - the prevalence of magnetic fields from power lines.

After the nuclear accident at Chernobyl had spread radioactivity far and wide, he discovered that Earth's already weakened natural energy resonance systems were either extinguished or severely damaged, and that it was resonance chaos that ruled. Two years later, he learnt that "A person with a highly ordered individual field, may force upon disorganised fields a chain reaction which has an organising effect on water. The water energy then starts to restore itself."

His research lead him to think that nature has developed two ways of protecting lifeforms against radiation, and these he calls 'rock dust technology' and 'humus medicine'. Certain rock dusts, or mixtures of rock dust, says Graefe, are able to hold off unwanted radiowaves, microwaves, infra-red radiation, light waves, ultra-violet, roentgen and gamma radiation; while humus molecules hold all the information necessary for healthy plants to grow.

"We have confused planet Earth with conflicting energies, which the natural system is not equipped to deal with. By imparting intelligent information through resonant materials balance can be restored," explains Barry Oldfield.

To counteract the harmful effects of radiation, Graefe discovered that natural energy flows in eco-systems can be stimulated by different kinds of rock dusts and special organic materials. He selected points at very old trees and tree stumps, with the aid of dowsing, to place homeopathic doses of rock dusts, composts and other healing agents, in a form of 'Earth acupuncture' treatment. These types of treatments were also applied in various ways to waterbodies, where they had great cleansing and energising effects.

To understand what was going on, Graefe developed his 'Resonance Method for Scientific Research' in 1988-89. It is basically energy dowsing using specially selected basalt rock from St Pauls Mountain, an old volcano in eastern Austria, as a pendulum. Now people are taught to use the pendulum so that they can work out which rock dusts and mixtures are appropriate for their soils. Organic and biodynamic farming "keeps up the local energy transfers in the landscape, but purely traditional practices are not enough to keep up with modern technological interference," he stressed.

After Graefe's death his colleague Dr Maria Felsenreich carried on the work, along with other members of the European Group for the Study and Elimination of Electro-magnetic Disturbances in Landscapes and Settlements. They believe that water, common to all life, carries a certain natural resonance, which, if disturbed, causes all life forms to suffer.

'Earth acupuncture'

Water that is active within the biosphere they call the 'water household'. Water is a carrier of information which can be contaminated by chemical pollution, electro-magnetic disturbance and atomic radiation. It had been found that one could "reprogram water bodies to adjust to disturbances with relatively small inputs of selected rock dusts and humus materials in carefully selected places, in a kind of terrestial acupuncture". This information is then transmitted quickly, often over large areas, through the antenna effect of trees and their link with underground waterbodies.

Treatments of great simplicity have been devised. For the protection of trees they advocate the burying of ten kilos of fresh or one year old grape remains in a hole, with at least one hole per hectare (2.2 ac) of forest. In parks, one egg shaped artificial stone is buried between tree roots, and in plantations and orchards these stones are placed at the beginning of tree rows. For grasslands granite dust is used to strengthen plant roots, and on cropping land it is spread at a rate of 3 tonnes to the hectare (one and a half tons to the acre).

Farmers can raise the water table, they find, by soaking 5kg of grape remains in 20lt water (12lbs in 4 gallons) for 12 hours. The brown liquid is poured out over a spot where plants have greatest vitality.

Communication towers, says the group, can sicken people and make animals aggressive or ill and plants suffer. To counteract the energy disturbance from them in residential areas they recommend spreading rock dust in ponds and vegetable beds. In compost they suggest adding it at 8 kg per cubic metre (18lbs per square yard) of heap.

For computer radiation protection they recommend people wear neck bags of rock dust - especially children, people with weak immune systems and young drug addicts, for which computer irradiation is most dangerous. (Studies have also shown that dangerous interactions occur when people taking psychiatric drugs are exposed to computer radiation.)

In addition to these methods, I think that our society needs to ask the question – do our kids really benefit from being exposed to computers from an early age, as is the fashion in schools? Not only does this lock up large amounts of financial resources, but it exposes kids to radiation at an age when the most damage may be done. It simply is not necessary to start young, as older students can learn to use them with ease.

I also question the educational value of computers. Do they actually stimulate learning processes? It has been found in studies that the use of musical instruments in schools is an excellent means of developing intelligence, as its forges a great many neural networks in the brain for enhanced mental ability. Computers, on the other hand, may be churning out mere robots from the education system. I think the emphasis on them in schools could be severely curbed, and the money saved redirected into musical studies and equipment.

Australia's Natural Resonance Study Group

At the invitation of Barry Oldfield, president of the very active WA branch of the Men of the Trees group, Dr Felsenreich, Dr Alexander Fries-Tersch and Monica Gassner visited Western Australia in January 1995 to share their ideas. This visit was said to have given "one of the most challenging notions for researchers to consider - that global changes to background radiation as a result of technological developments over the past 60 years have adversely affected plant health, which homeopathic treatments with rock dust and selected humus materials might be able to correct".

Soon after their visit a group was formed to conduct research and install various corrective devices in that part of the world. The Natural Resonance Study Group, one of several groups working on these problems around the world, is still going strong, with many subsequent visits by the Austrians and return visits by members going to Austria. Various corrective devices, mostly based on rock dusts, have been made and installed. There are rocket shaped cylinders for atmospheric protection, cone shaped stones for protection of resonance structures in ground waters and triangular shaped bags of rock dust to wear against computer radiation.

The Bio-Resonating Compost Heap (now called the Bio-Resonating Ring) is a donut shaped ring of composting materials specially selected: Marri gum leaves pre-rotted, grape remains and rock dust. In the middle a 'Tesla cylinder' is buried, to remove any electro-magnetic disturbance and on top of this are placed two egg shaped artificial stones, programmed to 'fix' the information which the mature humus imparts for the benefit of plants.

Dr Felsenreich claims that these heaps are instrumental in realigning and strengthening the magnetic fields of an area. She also states that they have had a 'water raising force'. When installed in Europe, in very dry forests and gardens, moist patches of soil have appeared. (Artificial radiation in the environment, she says, leads to aridity.)

A Bio-Resonating Ring inside a protective fence in Perth, WA.

Natural Resonance group member Kevin Dixon said in a 1997 newsletter that these rings "attract a dome of water beneath them, as well as creating an energy vortex around them". My own map dowsing of their effects has shown a wide reaching field of subtle energy influence emanating from them. However, when airports are nearby the beneficial fields are unable to penetrate these zones of excessive radiation. The energy fields also peter out when they reach the Indian Ocean.

In August 1998 Gary de Piazzi told me about the effects of installing numerous bio-resonating rings by the group. Members had reported their observations, which may lack scientific rigour, but nonetheless could not be dismissed. They have enjoyed a more tranquil atmosphere in the vicinity of the ring, and say how pleasant it is to sit near these installations. Stress is reduced and calmness prevails. Some report healing being facilitated and accelerated. Plants tend to be more vibrant looking, with glossier leaves. Bird life in the vicinity tends to increase. At Gary's place black cockatoos came to feed in the Marri gums after the ring went in- something that had never happened in 7 years there.

It was also noted by members that the bio-resonating rings that have the most beneficial effects are those that have had the most human attention, with people joining hands around them and giving them love.

The next generation of 'field stabilising' and 'pulse correcting devices' developed by the Austrians and used in WA was the Bio-Energetic Stabiliser, which also creates a beneficial energy field.

The BES comprises a special compost heap in a wooden box that's lined with aluminium mesh. Layers of green waste and grape remains are sprinkled with rock dust and worms and their castings. Air and water must be able to penetrate the heap, but not too much.

At the heart of the box is placed the Bio-Energetic Stabiliser stone, made from a special blend of various types and grades of rock dusts, plus potentised water and homeopathic essences, mixed with a specially selected cement and cast into a truncated conical shape. This stone provides the 'heartbeat' and acts as a carrier wave for all the information in the BES.

The BES is then left under or nearby the tallest tree in the yard to strengthen and amplify its influence. As the compost shrinks, more green or kitchen waste can be added to top it up. After 12 months the contents can be spread around the garden and the box refilled again in subsequent years.

After NRSG member Shelagh Williams installed a BES in her backyard a tree which had never flowered before blossomed beautifully, while other plants and her hens showed increased vigour and health.

Another member Max Scott reported, in Feb 1999, that the compost retrieved from his BES had been of the highest quality, with a profuse number of lively worms in it.

References:

1 - 'Secrets of the Soil', Christopher Bird and Peter Tompkins, Harper and Row, 1989.
2 - Men of the Trees Report no. 7, Barry Oldfield, March 1995.

Much of the information in this chapter has been extracted from newsletters and information provided by the

Above- Malcolm Borgward makes a BES in Perth, watched by Barry Oldfield on left and other workshop participants, February 1999.

Natural Resonance Study Group, *c/o secretary, PO Box 1453, Fremantle, 6160, WA, Australia. Membership is open to all.*

Maria Felsenreich is the co-ordinator of the **European Research Group for the Exploration and Elimination of Electromagnetic Disturbances in Landscapes and Settlements**, *address: Forschungsstelle fur Bioenergie, Hochwaldstrabe 37,Gartnerhof, A-2230, Ganserndorf-Sud, Austria.*

NRSG member and president of the Men of the Trees **Barry Oldfield** *has been documenting their work, both in WA and Europe, and made several videofilms on the benefits of using rock dusts, some with David Bellamy. Contact him at 3 Over Ave Lesmurdie WA 6076, ph 08 92916619.*

PART TWO : DOWSING and GARDENING

2:1 The Art of Dowsing

Dowsing is the ancient art of obtaining information about the unknown, of seeking lost objects or people, and tuning into unseen energies. It uses multi-sensory perception, often remote from its target, that is amplified by such tools as the classic forked stick, rods and pendulum.

Divining, radiesthesia, water witching and radionics are some of the terms that refer to various forms of dowsing. Country people are familiar with the local diviner seeking underground water or minerals with a twig or wires. What is less well known is the wide scope of its modern use. For there are limitless applications of dowsing.

Many naturopaths and a growing number of doctors and veterinarians all find dowsing to be a helpful diagnostic aid, and in countries such as the USA (where medical dowsing is frowned upon) the application of dowsing to agriculture (often in the form of radionic analysis and broadcasting) has become more and more popular in the last few years.

For a 'stone age' farmer, checking out the geomancy/energies of place or crop requirements - dowsing is an invaluable tool.

Dowsing harnesses our intuition, our gut feelings. We all experience intuition, but for any usefulness we need to put a handle on its often symbolic and mysterious communications. Dowsing provides a simple decoding system and allows intuition to become on-tap. It offers a key to controlled psychic self-development and helps forge a connection with one's higher self. This is probably the best treasure any dowsing can find.

Dowsing also harnesses our natural ability to sense electro-magnetic energies, from body and Earth energies, to radiation from man made sources - and the modern world is a mine-field of these.

> *"I know very well that many scientists consider dowsing as they do astrology, as a type of ancient superstition. According to my conviction this is, however, unjustified.*
>
> *The dowsing rod is a simple instrument which shows the reaction of a human nervous system to certain factors which are unknown to us at this time."*   **Albert Einstein, 1946.** [1]

How does dowsing work?

Someone with good insight to this question is the French Professor Yves Rocard, who has been studying magnetic reception and the mechanics of dowsing, much to the ridicule of his peers. When Rocard's article 'New Light on Magnetic Healing and the Action of the Dowsing Pendulum' was published in 'La Recherche', equivalent to the Scientific American) in January 1984, this heralded the light of its new acceptance in French scientific circles.

In his article Rocard (retired chief of the physics laboratory of the Ecole Normal, Paris, and the author of 'The Dowser's Signal', 1964) tells of the discovery of magnetic receptors in the body. Tiny magnetite crystals are found clustered in our brow ridges, adrenal glands and certain articulations of the vertebrae. These, he argues, are crucial receptors in the dowsing response, responsible for the 'sixth sense'. [2]

Other scientists have established the presence of tiny magnetite crystals in the heads and bodies of bacteria, honey bees, homing pigeons and fish. According to research at the University of California, whales and dolphins also use such receptors for their survival. Geomagnetic information compared with computerised recordings of cetacean sightings has shown that, over long distances, these animals prefer to travel along magnetic troughs that run for vast distances from north to south along the ocean floor. Strandings are most likely to occur at local magnetic low points.

Living within the background of the Earth's magnetic field also appears to stabilise the human sense of direction and timing. Without its influence our body's equilibrium is disturbed. This happened in the early manned space flights, after which low-level magnetic generators were fitted in space capsules.

We are all sensitive to electro-magnetic radiation in varying degrees. Oversensitivity to EMR can cause illness, because, although magnetism has beneficial applications in healing, excessive exposure can be deadly. Dr Cyril Smith of Salford University has studied the chronic health problems of the inhabitants of the Dorset (UK) village of Fishpond, where high voltage power lines straddle the town.

Smith found a pattern of widespread EMR, allergic reactions - with headaches, fatigue, insomnia, depression, flashes before the eyes and blackouts being common. More recently, studies in Bristol have concluded that high rates of lung cancer downwind from high voltage power lines are a consequence of air pollutant particles becoming 'sticky' in the EMR fields, and delivering much higher doses when breathed in.

The dowsers' art

Dowsing may be explained in terms of energy interaction. One explanation is that all matter radiates a weak but unique electromagnetic energy field around it. Dowsing allows us to detect the individual energy signature of a chosen object. Modern science has dubbed the art – the 'bio-resonance method'.

Mentally focusing on the object ('tuning in'), by such means as visualisation, the dowser resonates with it, a bit like radar. When the object is subsequently detected, resonance passes via the EMR-sensitive pineal and adrenal glands to the muscles involved with dowsing. This causes involuntary muscular contraction and the dowsing tool thus responds, often in pronounced twists and turns.

"The rod or pendulum is a read-out device of a mind state in resonance with the wave form of the cherished target." [3]

Dowsers find that they cannot easily dowse in an EMR polluted environment. Rural living and ocean voyages, on the other hand, are beneficial. The period of the waning moon is traditionally deemed appropriate for divination; while some dowsers report dizziness and an inability to dowse when the moon or sun is setting. At noon, when solar radiation is maximum, dowsing ability is also said to fade. Prof. Rocard reports that no dowsers are found at the magnetic equator.

This could be because where the north and south magnetic fields of the Earth meet there may be a neutral energy zone, similar to that found in a magnet.

Other factors reported to inhibit dowsing ability (by altering dowsers' energy fields) include the presence of positive ions (common in the atmosphere of artificial environments), illness, bad moods, intoxication, skeptical onlookers and the wearing of rings, watches and metals. Not all dowsers are affected by these factors though.

Virtually anyone can become a dowser. Especially if they are prepared to discard barriers of mental conditioning and learn to sense through the child within. This way one relearns to experience life afresh, directly contacting its power and mystery. Dowsers have simply enhanced their natural sensitivity with training and practise.

> *"Dowsing rods do not themselves find treasures.*
> *The magic rods move only in sensitive hands"* Goethe.

Dowsing and brain waves

Scientists have gained insight into the nature of altered states of awareness by measuring brain wave patterns with the electro-encephalograph (EEG). The EEG records brain rhythms in four frequency ranges, and these are known as alpha, beta, theta and delta waves.

Alpha waves, at 8 - 13 hertz (cycles per second) were the first to be discovered and are associated with a peaceful, meditative state. Beta waves range between 13 - 30 Hz and characterise normal waking activity. Theta waves, at 4 - 7 Hz, are associated with lucid dreaming, inspiration, hypnosis, spiritual reverie and access to unconscious mind. While delta waves, typical of deep sleep and the mind reaching far outwards, range from 0 - 4 Hz.

However some yogis' and psychics' brain waves don't even register on the EEG, presumably because they are operating at different frequencies to the norm. The Russians have discovered a new brain frequency, called 'ultra-theta', which they say can go around the world in seconds and perhaps acts as a carrier wave for telepathic communications.

A sophisticated version of the EEG, the Mind Mirror registers the action of each brain hemisphere simultaneously. For 6 years Mind Mirror originator Geoff Blundell and Maxwell Cade tested over 3,000 people, including yogis, psychics, meditators and psychic healers. He found that different states of mind correspond to various brain wave patterns.

Cade was fascinated by what he called a 'Fifth State' pattern, associated with lucid awareness, cosmic consciousness, illumination, nirbikalpa samadhi etc. This Fifth State is characterised by a symmetrical use of the two brain hemispheres and activity in all brain frequencies except delta. In the rare individuals who maintain this state constantly, a life of joy, deep gratitude for being alive and concern for the welfare of others are the factors in common with them.

Studies with the EEC reveal that when a psychic healer is healing they exhibit the Fifth State. This state is then induced to the brain of the subject who is not normally capable of it. A person's healing ability correlates with the amplitude, symmetry, and most importantly, the stability of this Fifth State. [4]

Dr Edith Jurka tested many talented dowsers with the Mind Mirror and found that they exhibited a brain wave pattern similar to the Fifth State. The difference being that dowsers have increased beta activity (from the intense concentration involved) and also a high delta amplitude (indicating a search pattern). A few master dowsers are able to maintain this state constantly. In Jurka's understanding:

> *"Dowsing is an expansion of lucid awareness, in essence familiarity in communication with the Universal Intelligence".*

The mastery of altered states is heralding a new age of intelligence, where wisdom is derived from thought that blends rationality with intuition. As Dr Jurka sees it:

> *"Bilateral brain symmetry is central to health control in general."* [5]

We can achieve greater wellbeing when mentally balanced, our intuitive mind harnessed. It's easy, if we choose to experience the realisation of unity, be sensitised to life and open to the mysteries of the universe.

Dowsing is a wonderful exercise of holistic thinking and sensing, that brings many personal and environmental benefits.

Dowsing with the Pendulum

The pendulum is my instrument of choice when dowsing. It is easy to carry around and may be worn as a pendant, for greater accessibility and discretion. It is also a more versatile tool.

The pendulum's rotations and oscillations can be used to convey answers to questions. These are first self-programmed and practised until the system has lodged in the subconscious mind. Then the intuition can have free rein as the pendulum opens the mental doorways.

What to use as a pendulum? Any small roundish or tear shaped object capable of being attached to a thread and hang straight will work. It could be a seed pod, wooden bob, or stone pendant. Some gardeners have been known to pull up a radish and dangle it from garden string! Even a soggy tea bag can work!

However the best thing is a quartz crystal, fastened with either silver, copper or gold (as these metals are good conductors of subtle energy).

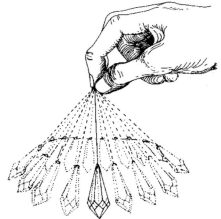

Crystal pendulums

Quartz crystal has an extraordinary ability to focus, amplify, transmute, store and channel energies, as well as sensitise people's psychic awareness. Quartz can provide a link between our world and that of the nature spirits, by facilitating our communications with them.

In ancient Hopi Indian legend quartz crystal, chief of the mineral tribe, said

52

"I will help human beings see the origin of disease. I will heal the mind. I will help to bring wisdom and clarity in dreams."

Many people today are using crystals to stimulate their consciousness, for heightened meditation, energy balancing, Earth healing and other purposes. Different types of crystals are suited to different uses.

When acquiring a crystal pendulum allow the intuitive mind to do the selection. Take that which 'grabs you' on the first impression, or use another pendulum to select one.

Avoid the artificial lead glass 'crystal' that is often sold. These can be identified by their exaggerated rainbow colour effects and air bubbles which are often apparent. You may decide upon several crystals of different colours and use them for different purposes.

Natural clear quartz channels strong positive (yang) energy and is a good choice for a pendulum. However too much yang energy can make a sensitive dowser over-stimulated and the clear quartz is best not to be worn all the time. A better choice in this case might be a cloudy, yin type crystal. This type can help develop intuitive powers. Meditating with a yin crystal held in the left hand can aid intuition, it is said.

Amethyst quartz is purple, a colour that combines yin and yang qualities. It has a particularly good ability to balance and harmonise energies and is a favourite of geomancers.

Smoky quartz, of a brown to black hue, tends to affect the astral/ emotional body, helping to draw out negativity from it. Other gems suited to pendulums are moonstone, lazurite, peridot, and zircon.

After acquiring a new crystal pendulum you can consecrate it for your own use. You might hold it to your heart and visualise loving golden energy pouring into it. Ask if it will help you with your dowsing work and thank it when you have finished.

Occasionally you will need to cleanse the crystal of any acquired negativity. This can be done by washing it under running water for a few minutes, leaving it in full moonlight or purely by mind power.

Hold the crystal and visualise a cleansing process, such as holding it under a waterfall or waves, or wiping a blackboard clean.

When to dowse

Only begin a dowsing session when you're comfortable and relaxed, and not distracted. Get into a mind state of passive concentration and calm detachment from the process, without conditioned or wishful thought interfering. Experience the subtle and mysterious with fresh eyes! An initial period of meditation or self-hypnosis may be helpful in slowing down the analytical mind and increasing alpha wave levels.

How to get started

Attach your pendulum to a 20 cm (8") length of string, the end of which has been securely wrapped around the index finger of your dominant hand. Give the pendulum a small push until it swings easily up and down, away from you. This oscillating movement is called the 'neutral' position, and is used to get the pendulum started, for in-between questions, or as a 'don't know' indication.

Initially you can use thought power to direct the pendulum's movements. Learn to will the oscillating pendulum to rotate one direction, return to neutral, rotate the other way, then return back to neutral. Practise these movements several times, until they become smooth and effortless. When the movements slow down, give the pendulum a little push while it is oscillating.

If nothing happens, don't worry and don't try too hard. Put the pendulum away and try at another time. Sometimes an experienced dowser can help by touching you on the shoulder as you try.

If you are still not confident with polarity dowsing try swinging the pendulum, in oscillation, over the terminals of a battery. Note which direction it rotates over each terminal, as an indication of what your positive and negative responses should be.

Generally speaking, right handed people get a clockwise rotation for positive and anti clockwise for negative; left handed responses are visa-versa. The positive polarity corresponds to masculine, yang qualities and 'yes', whilst the negative is equated with feminine, yin energy and 'no'.

The author dowses for ley lines on Queensland's Sunshine Coast.

A weak or wobbly 'yes' or 'no' may indicate a need to reframe a question, or that the time is not right to dowse.

It is best to choose clear, unambiguous questions for real problem solving and experiments that can provide instant feedback. Repetitive games are not suitable, as the intuitive processes switch off when bored.

Begin a dowsing session by asking if the time is suitable, the question appropriate, or if you have permission to know the answer. A good starting question could be -

"May I / Should I ask this question right now?"

Double check your results at a later time. Never be in a hurry and don't dowse for more than 10 minutes before having a break. Dowsing is very tiring, due to intensive concentration required. If you dowse when you're tired - results can be unreliable.

Energy dowsing

Life force (also knowns as ch'i, orgone, prana, odic force, vril etc) can be 'read' by the pendulum. You mentally attune to the type of energy sought, then start the pendulum oscillating in the neutral position before approaching a likely energy field. When the pendulum begins to rotate, indicating that resonance has been achieved, the angle and velocity of the rotations will give an indication of the measure of force involved.

The number of rotations that occur before oscillations resume can also be counted. This measuring technique is known as 'finding the serial number'. For better efficiency you can pre-program the pendulum to give a number of rotations out of 10 or 100.

This technique can be usefully applied to health analysis and vitality monitoring. You pendule over the palm of the hand for an indication of energy levels, finding the serial number.

Another energy monitoring technique uses a simple ruler. Taking the top end to represent the peak of health, one scans down from it with the free index finger and the pendulum oscillating, until rotations start up. The number dowsed will indicate the degree of deviation from health.

Or you can take the middle of the ruler to represent optimum health or condition, the top end to indicate over-active (hyper-) conditions, and the lower half to indicate under-active (hypo-) conditions.

Using samples

When seeking something, beginners may need to physically hold a sample of it, in order to feel better attuned to the task. Some dowsers call these samples 'witnesses'. A person's witness acts as a permanent and current link between them and the dowser, no matter the distance apart, or when the witness was taken. For instance, you can practise remote health dowsing with witnesses and regularly check healing processes at your convenience.

The pendulum is either swung over the sample while posing questions, or it can be held in the free hand while dowsing with the other. Some

Workshop participants dowse over samples of rock dust. A mystery light appeared above a mini Power Tower when film was processed!

56

people use a hollow pendulum to accommodate witnesses.

Food dowsing is a means of gaining familiarity with the pendulum and samples. Food samples may be checked for compatability with oneself, in the kitchen or the shop. This is a basic technique - establishing the harmony or disharmony between things. A principle which can also be applied in the garden, with companion planting selections, for instance.

Simple questions such as 'Is this food good for me?' can be posed. With negative responses your questions can be more specific, such as 'Am I allergic to the item?', or 'Are chemical residues or toxin levels high?'. Work slowly and concentrate carefully on each item.

Chart dowsing

After practice, your ability to visualise or conceptualise something can replace the need for a physical sample to be present. Simply write the name of the thing, person or concept on a piece of paper and dowse over that. Groups of words can be arranged together as a dowsing chart.

Charts can be simple lists, or words arranged in a protractor (fan) shape. Until familiarity is established with the chart one mentally reads it out, word by word. When you are more experienced, the pendulum will initially oscillate over the middle of the base line, then gradually alter its oscillation angle to point to the appropriate word.

Rates method

A quick ritual of mental attunement is established by altering the length of the pendulum's string. Whilst the pendulum swings in neutral, the target object is mentally concentrated upon and the full length of string is slowly shortened until rotations commence.

Then the string is wrapped securely around the finger and the pendulum will now only rotate when encountering the object of the exercise (be it physical, abstract or conceptual). It's a bit like putting blinkers on.

Using this encoding technique you can seek things in a more methodical way. T. C. Lethbridge invented the system and applied fixed values to the rates, assuming that everyone else should get the same rate as his.

With a more flexible approach you will find that rates can change over time and everyone's rate for something can be different.

Time

Don't be restricted by the present time. Delve back in time to assist the prognosis of a problem. Investigate your past lives. Or mentally project forward into the future. Apparently there's less psychic interference in future time!

If you need to check a time scale, save your energy by finding a broad range of times, then narrowing down the possibilities. For example, ask 'Did whatever I need to know happen in the last half century?' 'Was it over 30 years ago?' 'Was it between 40 and 50 years ago?' etc.

Body Dowsing

There are many body reflexes that can be developed to indicate a dowsing response. These may be stomach aches, muscular tension, tics, a throbbing along the meridians, yawns and even hiccups. The whole body may sway from side to side. Or a tingling sensation may be felt in the finger or hands.

The index finger might be pointed at the target, or the hands held out in front with palms outwards or pointed downwards. The thumb and forefinger may be rubbed together, until a rough feeling denotes the response. This is something like the 'stick' reaction of the rubber stick pad in some radionic systems.

Blink dowsing was first recorded by an eighteenth century clergyman, Daniel Wilson, who found that he blinked spontaneously over underground water. He then applied the technique to mentally posed questions and his blinking would always indicate 'yes'.

One Englishwoman gazes at an electronic light when posing questions, causing it to swing forwards and backwards for yes and left to right for a no. Channelling energy through the eyes is the likely mechanism for such telekinesis.

"One of the most important things you can learn in dowsing is that the aim is not - as it is in the more conventional sciences - to build ever

bigger and more complicated crutches, but rather to move towards absolute simplicity. And what could be simpler than using yourself?"
English dowser Tom Graves (who now lives in Victoria, Australia).

Poor results

Poor results can be caused by a negative attitude of the dowser or someone close by; inability to change to an appropriate state of consciousness or to concentrate; haste; fatigue; lack of confidence or subject familiarity; preconceived thinking; lack of enthusiasm; unethical or vague questioning and lack of permission to know.

The scepticism of observers is a well-known hindrance to successful dowsing. The expectation of some personal benefit to the dowser may also wreck results.

Ghostly etheric patterns left behind by things, called 'remanence', and stray thought forms (mind projections) can confuse dowsing. These can be dispelled mentally, for example by visualising a powerful laser ray emanating from the palm of your hand, directed to the problem area.

Asking the correct question is all-important. It often must be intuitively derived. The more knowledge of a subject, the better you are equipped to ask the right question, however intuition can triumph over ignorance!

Dowsing and Soil testing

Dowsing can be a wonderful tool to assist the eco-farmer and gardener. The viability of seeds can be checked. Compatibility of soil and plants can be determined by placing samples half a metre (18") apart on a sheet of paper and penduling between them. By placing fertilisers at a third point in relation to the samples, creating a triangular arrangement, one can test whether compatibility or growth may be improved by various combinations (see diagram next page).

Degrees of compatibility or soil improvements can also be tested with a soil witness and scale measure. This method can compare the effectiveness of possible inputs. When a number has been divined for an existing soil / plant combination, a written list of fertilisers/soil additives is checked through to see which ones may improve the rating.

Another way is to first tune in to your soil, then point to various plants to find the most compatable. You can also use dowsing to check for affinities between certain plants (companion planting), between plants and animals, plants and soil pH, etc. When planting special trees it's a good idea to check whether the location suits them, as radiations might stunt growth in geopathic zones.

When certain elements are lacking in soil, it is better to apply them, if possible, in the form of compost, rather than as single additives. The soil may then be able to balance itself naturally. According to Rudolph Steiner, and other authorities more recently, soil bacteria act as the alchemists of the garden and if certain elements are lacking, they have the ability to transmute other elements to ones needed for balance.

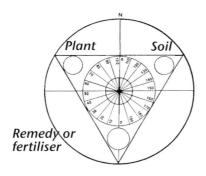

Diagram: To test for soil/ plant compatibility, or the value of soil inputs - place samples and swing the pendulum over the centre point, asking it to oscillate at an angle over the correct degree of measure.

The Story of Ralph Thomas

Tasmania's most celebrated dowser was the late Ralph Thomas of Leith. Ralph's speciality was soil analysis. He could determine soil composition, which elements were available to plants and which were 'locked up'; those needed to grow certain crops and in what quantity.

His method was to spread 70 bottles of various nutritive substances on the ground while holding a crop and soil sample in one hand. Using a Y rod he then dowsed over the bottles to find which were suitable and thus he advised insurance clients on what products they needed.
Quickly the word of his successes spread and he was in great demand. He gave up his insurance job and turned to professional dowsing. He tested soils throughout Tasmania and the rest of Australia, twice

travelling to England to give lectures to the British Society of Dowsers, and also wrote articles for their journal.

An English farmer in Cheshire who was having trouble growing anything sent Ralph a scale plan of the farm, over which he passed his divining rod. In this way he determined soil deficiencies and remedies at a distance. He also used and advocated 'radiesthetic coils' of copper wire strategically placed around the farm to improve energies. As a result the farm bloomed.

Ralph was keen on organic growing and helped man a busy soil testing stand at the Organic '78 and '79 Festivals. He was well ahead of his time in advocating healthy soil as a prerequisite of healthy life.

From the start he had also practised health divination, believing that illness can be measured in the vitality of an organ. He selected medicines to restore balance, refusing to call it 'curing'.

Ralph received letters from people the world over seeking diagnosis. They sent their blood, hair or hand writing samples for analysis. Not understanding the mechanism at work, he just accepted that it did work.

Ralph also diagnosed and treated noxious 'Earth rays' (geopathic zones), utilising many different gadgets and techniques to de-ray houses and animal pens. Recognising that there are also beneficial Earth energies, he found one noteworthy place that fairly made your hair stand on end and where, at age 92, the farmer was still milking cows.

In his estimation, 80% of people have potential in dowsing and he encouraged many to try, including a few apprentices who he was glad to teach when satisfied their interest was genuine.

At the time of his death, on July 12th 1979, aged 78, he was running weekly classes in homoeopathy for 30 people.

Ralph once stated: *"I may not have really examined the ethics of dowsing, but I always felt the only thing wrong was when it was used for things like gambling and financial gain. I am dealing with natural things and can't feel there is anything wrong with using my natural talents. I think it might be more wrong if I did not."*

Ralph's capacity and knowledge carries on in the work of Ross Henderson, who practises the humanistic approach to dowsing that his teacher instilled. Ross reported in 1985:

> *"I have run my farm basically by radionics for 8 years now and the health of stock and crops still amazes."*

Ross formed the Ralph Thomas Radiesthetic Society soon after the master's death, with Ralph's homoeopathic students. [6]

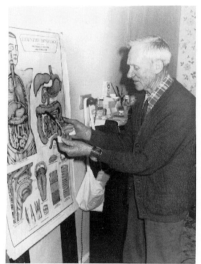

Ralph Thomas practicing health divination. Photo courtesy Hobart Mercury.

Pendulums and Gardening

Ann Miller, a member of the Natural Resonance Study group, has described her use of the pendulum in gardening.

Ann always starts her inquiries with 'Can I?'/'Should I?/May I? followed by a clearing of her own energies, centering herself, opening herself to the work and asking for guidance and protection.

The most appropriate site for a specific plant in the garden can be divined directly in the garden, or by map dowsing, whichever is most convenient, she says. Ann has developed a detailed general broadcast program that clearly outlines her intent in regards to how plants should grow, what protection they may need from pests, disease and artificial disturbances, as well as asking for assistance from the various nature spirits and devas. This written intent is placed between two sheets of black paper, along with another page identifying the boundaries of her property. On the top sheet, a diagram of a transmitter is placed.

To activate the transmitter, the open ends of the two lines are joined with a pencil line. To deactivate, the pencil line is erased.

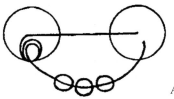

Ann Miller's transmitter symbol.

As an alternative, a crystal can be used to accept and broadcast the program. Ask the pendulum for the most appropriate crystal and whether it is large enough to accept the program, as well as transmit it. The crystal can then be placed in the garden, having determined the most appropriate position with the pendulum.

By creating a checklist of all the possible maladies a plant can suffer, from diseases to nutrient deficiencies and soil conditions, the pendulum can be used as a diagnostic tool. Similarly, a list can be made of all the possible soil amendments, for dowsing a suitable fertiliser program.

Ann suggests that in the beginning it does help to have actual samples of the materials and these can be stored in small vials or containers such as film canisters. The effectiveness of a dowsed program can then be tested by grouping selected samples and then dowsing the vitality levels of the plant with and without them.

As an alternative to pesticides Ann has used specially programmed crystals to keep pests away from her crops. By using such a crystal, Ann has managed to keep slaters away from her strawberries, allowing her and Dave to eat their own home grown strawberries for the very first time. [7]

References-

1 - From a letter to H. G. Peisach from Albert Einstein, Feb. 1946, American Society of Dowsers Journal May 1982.
2 - American Society of Dowsers Journal, May 1984
3 - T. Edward Ross, ASD Journal, Feb. 1986.
4 - 'The Awakened Mind - Biofeedback and the Development of Higher States of Awareness', Dr Maxwell Cade.
5 - 'Brain Characteristics of Dowsers', Dr Edith Jurka, British Society of Dowsers Journal, December 1983.
6 - Ross Henderson, PO Forth, Tasmania, 7310, ph 03 6428 2353.
7 - Nov. '99 newsletter of the Natural Resonance Study Group.

2:2 Radionics and Beyond

Radionics is a system of analysing and affecting energies at a distance through the medium of dowsing and energetic ability of the operator. It is used for human and animal health and is most popular in its agricultural applications. In its current form it has been around for almost 100 years.

Mayan Radionic Agriculture

Radionics wasn't so much a product of 20th century thinking as, perhaps, an echo of ancient understandings of vanished cultures that have been largely lost in the passage of time. Christopher Bird has written about an ancient Central American system that both Steiner and radionics practitioners would have had no trouble in comprehending. [1]

Intrepid traveller Gabriel Howearth, Bird writes, discovered Mayan people in the Central American jungle, who had vast farms, some over 400 acres in size, thriving in the midst of tropical weeds and pests. These permaculture farms were highly polycultural, with much diversity and intercropping, and it had fruit and nut trees over a thousand years of age. Howearth was let into the tribes' confidence and they demonstrated their techniques, which merged an incredible knowledge of astronomy/astrology with geomancy and radionics, to achieve perfect pest control.

It has been well documented and corroborated that the Maya people had contact with the Egyptians long ago and this could help explain their accurate knowledge, still to be seen carved in stone calendars. Their radionic pest control techniques involved tapping into specific cosmic forces at the right time and collecting and relaying these influences by tiny pyramids along the local grid of Earth energy lines.

The Mayans used small symbolic representations of the planets as well as glyphs for weeds or insects with the pyramids for controlling the pests. The glyphs for pests are carved next to the appropriate planet on the calendars. They knew, for instance, that Venus influenced ladybugs and Mars affected aphids. As the planets moved into appropriate positions, the glyphs and ash of weed seeds were placed in these pyramids, to allow the planetary energies to radiate the messages along the Earth energy lines, and thus effect control. Had the Mayan codices not been destroyed by Christian invaders we might know much more of their amazing radionic system.

Modern radionics

Radionics is a sophisticated system of dowsing that uses different tools, but the same sensitivities. That being so, the tools are naturally only as good as the operator! Radionics has a fascinating history.

In the early years of this century a brilliant American physician, Dr Albert Abrams, discovered that all matter radiates energy, and that the waves generated may be detected across space by human reflexes. He was expert at diagnosing disease states through the consistently dull sounds percussed at various reflex areas on people's bodies. Abrams set out to devise a wave-emitting instrument which could alter the character of these signals, cancel out and cure afflictions.

The Oscilloclast was thus developed with the help of a distinguished radio research engineer. It proved so successful that by 1919 he was teaching the use of the 'Abrams box' to other doctors. For his efforts in developing the science of radionics, Abrams was branded a quack by the threatened medical mafia. Those coming to his defence included Sir James Barr, past president of the British Medical Association, who described Abrams as 'the greatest genius in the medical profession.'

Medical radionics was eventually outlawed in the US, but it did gain acceptance in England where, in 1924, and sadly just after Abrams' death, a parliamentary committee of enquiry into radionic practice sanctioned its use. Later the Radionic Association formed to regulate its practice.

In agricultural radionics, pioneering work began in 1951, when engineer Curtis Upton teamed up with electronics expert William Knuth to experiment with pest control in the cotton fields of Tucson, Arizona. Using a radionic box the size of a radio, an aerial photo of 1800 hectares (4000 acres) of cotton belonging to one of the state's biggest growers and a remedy against the cotton pests, to act in a homoeopathic manner, they hoped to save the company $US30,000 annually on pesticides. The experiment worked. As a bonus the expected cotton yield increased by 25%, with 20% more seeding from the increased numbers of bees, plus a virtual absence of snakes.

Revelling in the success of subsequent experiments they teamed up with industrial chemist and inventor Howard Armstrong with the backing of General Henry M Gross to form a radionics company, UKACO Inc, which guaranteed 'no pest control, no pay'. This resulted in pesticide salesmen being turned away by farmers, some of whom were successfully doing the radionic treatments themselves. The chemical companies reacted by calling UKACO fraudulent and lobbied the Department of Agriculture to follow suit. A patent application was rejected. Farmers were brainwashed into also believing radionics to be fraudulent and so UKACO was eventually forced out of business, such was the threat that it posed the chemical economy. UKACO themselves never claimed 100% success, especially if there was interference from standing irrigation pipes, high tension electric wires, leaky transformers, wire fences, radar or certain soil conditions.

Young American radionics engineer T Galen Hieronymus fared better with his radionic devices at around the same time. Working more low key, the Hieronymus Machine gained its US patent in 1949 for the 'detection of emanations from materials and measurement of the volumes thereof' (with later patents in the UK and Canada). He then demonstrated its lethal capacity in an experiment. Selecting 3 ears of corn on which corn worms were munching he began treatment. After broadcasting for 10 minutes per hour around the clock for 3 days, 2 of the worms were reduced to mush and the third died 24 hours later. In awe of its deadly potential, Hieronymus would never reveal full details of his invention until serious researchers of impeccable character might show an interest.

In England in the 1930's Mr and Mrs de la Warr were also inventing radionic instruments. These broadcast healing to sick plants and radiant energy patterns of nutrients to the soil. By 1954 their treated cabbages were growing 3 times larger than average. One experiment was supervised by Dr E.W. Russell of Oxford University's agricultural department. A strip of land was divided into 10 plots. Five were chosen at random by Dr Russell, photographed before planting and then treated. After 3 weeks treatment, lettuce seedlings were planted and treatment continued for 12 more weeks, after which Dr Russell supervised weighing. The treated lettuces had more leaves, less mortality, were heavier and had an increased 32% in yield.

In 1956 they tried broadcasting nutritional energy to an inert substance, vermiculite, by blowing quantities in front of the radionic apparatus, then added this to a seed raising mix. Compared to control plants, results were fantastic and they were confirmed by a leading agricultural firm. The vermiculite crop of rye, cocksfoot and other plants was 186% heavier in moist weight, and protein was increased by 270%.

The Twyford Seeds company tried to duplicate these results without success, so the de la Warrs reasoned that a human factor was involved. To test for this they added plain vermiculite to potted oats and the assistants were told that it was treated. The untreated oats thrived above the others and, in demonstrating the effect of mind over matter, the de la Warrs considered this their most important experiment.

When radionically testing and broadcasting agricultural remedies, one can use a photo negative of the land concerned as a witness. Remedy witnesses, or symbols to represent them, are brought into contact with the photo negative for a certain period of time at regular intervals. Energies of the land, plants and pests can be re-programmed this way.

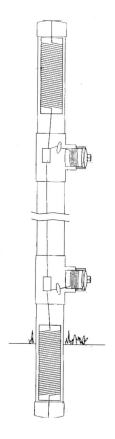

Cosmic Pipes

The twenty first century radionic farmer is just as likely to use a 'Cosmic Pipe' to broadcast homeopathic remedies, as their predecessors would have used a radionic box or glyph and pyramid in the past.

You can buy such a device straight off the shelf these days or build your own. Whatever the case, you need to have had some training and be able to dowse, as they cannot work on their own.

T. Galen Hieronymous was the American inventor of the original Cosmic Pipe, which consists of a PVC pipe fitted out with simple wiring circuitry and glass jars to hold remedy samples for broadcast. A simple resistor and diode circuit with biodynamic preps amplifies and broadcasts energy. Hieronymous found he had to make the pipe at least 2.1 m (8') high, to tap into the boundary of the Earthly and cosmic energies. Energies are channelled down into the soil and better crops grow this way.

The first models worked so well, that the earth forces overwhelmed the atmospheric fruiting forces and there was too much disease and pests.

The energy was imbalanced. This was corrected by a 2 way design and he used this to broadcast horn manure downwards and horn silica upwards. This worked very well. At last he had found a way to get the biodynamic preps out onto the land reliably and economically, with large areas easily covered.

These days, says Hugh Lovel, "broadcasting has come of age", with the regime of putting out the biodynamic preparations of horn manure with winter horn clay, and horn silica with summer horn clay, broadcast via the Cosmic Pipe continuously. Many agricultural problems have now been solved with this new age application of biodynamics. [2]

Cosmic Pipes have been used to detoxify and energise soil, crops and animal food. American researcher Don Mattioda has reported the repelling of mosquitoes in the USA and elephants from a Malaysian date palm orchard.

Ethics

Questions of ethics and boundaries have rightfully come into radionic debate, as its acceptance is widening globally after almost a century. Because we can affect something or someone remotely means having to maintain great integrity and care. An ethical person always dowses for permission, asking 'Can I, Should I, May I?' before doing any energy work.

Biodynamic farmer Barbara Hedley makes the point that the native Australian landscape does not appreciate European biodynamic remedies imposed upon it, with their very different energies. She recommends excluding those areas from not only BD spraying, but radionic broadcasts too, and suggests removing, or crossing out, any wild vegetation areas from maps or photos used as radionic witnesses. [3]

Simplified radionics

The radionics that developed around the middle of the 20th century had an emphasis on the material, with many variations on the Radionic Box developed, each carrying a high price tag. Later developments moved it into more ethereal realms. For instance, David Tansley introduced the etheric body energy systems for radionic health testing.

In Tansley's philosophy -   *'the analysis is the treatment'*.

This follows on from the old esoteric maxim, that -

'energy follows thought'.

The Box and witnesses are all props helping to focus the healers' attention and establish resonance with them, until healing is induced, he felt. Radionic practice is like ritual, the purpose of which is to accumulate and direct energy. If it is possible to reach this state unaided, then material props become unnecessary

Dowsers have found that they can effectively practise radionics by dowsing and broadcasting using simple charts and diagrams on sheets of paper - proving that intention is more important than hardware.

References:

1 - 'Secrets of the Soil', C Bird and P Tompkins, Harper and Row, 1989.
2 - 'Agricultural Renewal', Hugh Lovel, Union Agriculture Inst., 2000.
3 - 'Newsleaf', Journal of the Biodynamic Farmers & Gardeners Association of Australia, Dec. 2001, PO Box 54 Bellingen, ph/fax 02 6655 0566.
4 - 'Dowsing and Healing', Alanna Moore, 1995 (out of print).

For more information about radionics in Australia contact:
Gil Robertson
Principal of the Radionics Centre of Australia
P.O. Box 51
Port Lincoln SA 5606
email: gilrob@dove.net.au

2.3 *Plant energies*

An esoteric understanding of the subtle forces of nature is helpful for the sensitive eco-gardener and farmer in deepening their interactions with the landscape and all its lifeforms, seen and unseen.

The spiral force

There is an old esoteric maxim that ***'all is energy'***. This is now verified by science, but people like dowsers seem to be always several steps ahead of scientific knowledge!

Energy, time and space tends to curve and follow spiral patterns. The spiralling nature of energy is very apparent in the vegetable kingdom, and is seen in the unfurling of a fern frond and the twisting of a liana vine up a tree trunk. The tips of all plant organs (stem, tendril, root, flower, stalk) describe an irregular helical course, called by biologists 'nutation' (after the Latin - to nod) and by Charles Darwin 'an inborn oscillation'.

A dowser's model of plant energies, proposed by American T. Edward Ross, takes this one step further. According to Ross all plants, and each of their components, are enveloped by a spiral cone of force, its etheric blueprint. These cones, having a 52 ^{0} angle at their apex, are found in an ascending sequence of four.

The lowermost, a downward pointing cone, surrounds the root system. The second, pointing upwards, rests on this base to base, enclosing the upper part of the plant. Another energy diamond pattern is found attached to the first, point to point, to create a double diamond formation (pictured on right).

This quadripartite signature wave provides 2 counter-rotating spins, one more active than the other, to create a certain friction and imbalance that serves to generate creative growth. The energy pattern (aura) exists from seed and is easily located by dowsing. T.C. Lethbridge describes similar cones around people.

Kirlian photographs of seeds show the mature form of a plant's aura, and within its overall form exist infinite smaller energy pattern forms. In older plants this formative energy pattern becomes less distinct.

It is possible to reinforce a plant's helical spin to create perfect resonance by such means as sound, colour, electricity, light, heat, chemicals and the right mental note. The benefits of this are found to be unusually good soil conditions, good quality vegetable yields, and protection from insect and animal invasion. The method is simple.

In deep meditation one simply visualises placing a 4 part helical cone over every seed, seedling and garden plot, requesting the cone's reinforcement and its resonance with those waveforms natural to the location and each particular variety. This need only be made once - it will be active until the end of the growing season. [1]

'Fundamental ray'

Radionic pioneers the de la Warrs determined that every living plant has a critical rotational position (CRP) in relation to Earth's magnetic field. As seeds sprout in the ground they twist around until locked into this CRP, helping explain why direct-seeded plants do better than transplants.

If transplanted and also kept in CRP, plants thrive. To do so, mentally attune to the plant for a few moments. Then slowly rotate the plant pot around whilst pendulum dowsing with the other hand. When you have become accustomed to doing this, you can forget the pendulum and simply hold the pot and rotate the plant slowly and feel for the correct position intuitively. When a positive response is elicited, plant in exactly that orientation. For me there is a feeling of 'stickiness', of not wanting to turn further at the appropriate point. It's a good exercise in attunement.

Prior to this concept old-time dowsers delving into the subtle energies have spoken of the 'fundamental ray' and the 'front door' of plants, which may or may not be synonymous terms.

Like energy centre chakras in humans, the fundamental ray is a part of the plant's aura, where a concentrated stream of energy can be detected on both sides of the plant (although it is strongest on only one side).

The fundamental ray could be likened to the heart chakra or seat of consciousness of the plant. It can be felt by the sensitive scanning of hands held a short distance away from the tree. When hands scan over the 'front door' of the plant - sensations, such as a tingling of the hands, may be felt.

Many dowsers use coils or wires for plant healing that are positioned within this 'ray' for enhanced effectiveness.

The powers of trees

The natural forest is a power centre for the landscape. Trees play an important environmental role in acting like acupuncture needles. They are transmitters of subterranean Earth energies and moisture that's brought up to the surface, as well as being antennae for receiving beneficial cosmic energies from above. As in the 2 way energetic responses to human scale acupuncture - these intermediaries between Heaven and Earth establish a homeostasis, helping to maintain environmental health and wellbeing.

Trees moderate the climate and process minerals from deep down to ferti-

lise the surface. Humus from their leaves builds up a mineral rich colloidal insulating layer, an organic diffusion filter that separates the negatively charged ground from the positively charged atmosphere. The forest is also the 'cradle' of water, collecting and purifying it.

Some trees have an affinity for people. European tradition has it that oaks, the rowan, hawthorn, beech, hazel, apple and willow are very people-friendly. Unfriendly trees are said to be elder, elm, ash, holly, pine and fig. Gnarled and twisted trees are best avoided. To divine friendly or useful trees for yourself - make up a list or fan chart of all the trees that grow in your area and pendulum dowse for levels of affinity between you and the trees.

Some trees have healing qualities, apparent by the colour of their aura. These can be divined by dowsing with a colour chart. There are said to be 4 main useful colours. Green is good for general healing; blue, for meditation, creativity or calming; yellow for learning and mental stimulation; and white for cleansing and general purposes.

When discovering a new tree and approaching it - don't just rush in. Stand back and send love to it, mingling your energies together. Then step closer with your feeling hand extended and scan the tree's auric field. Continue until you find the 'heart chakra' of the tree, where sensations are most strongly felt. Mentally tune in to the tree. Ask to 'see' its colour. Ask if the tree colour/energy matches with your needs.

Green auras make good birthing trees. Expectant mothers can become familiar with the tree for some time beforehand and communicate lovingly with it. Eventually a 2 way flow of energy will develop. At birthing time lean against it and feel the calming, pain-dulling influence.

For general healing always lavish lots of love on your healing tree. When hugging a tree one's aura may extend to double its size after just 2 minutes and this can be very revitalising.

NSW Dowser Isabel Bellamy advocates placing small branchlets of dowsing-selected trees against your skin for a period, possibly overnight, to absorb healing energies from them directly.

Plant communication

Plants communicate in several ways. Roots send out chemical messages into the soil which determine whether they are friendly or not to other vegetation. Some maintain hostile territoriality, with toxic root exudates. They can become rampant, dominating weeds outside of their natural environment through this mechanism.

American physicist Ed Wagner reported his discovery of another communication system in early 1989. When a tree is chopped, he found, adjacent trees put out an electrical pulse. The chopped tree puts out a massive alarm

73

cry, detected by an electronic probe, and the others respond.

He calls this communication mode W-waves, being non-electromagnetic standing waves which travel about 1m/1yd per second through the trees and about 5 times that speed in air. These standing waves are continuously travelling up and down trees, the voltage going up and down as you go up the tree.

Song and dance

Plants respond well to music, especially to classical Bach, baroque and Indian sacred music. 'Sonic Bloom' is an innovative fertilising system whereby music corresponding to the dawn chorus of birds - which is a natural growth stimulant - is played to crops while a foliar fertiliser is applied. Plants absorb enormous amounts of the fertiliser when exposed to the music and grow to huge dimensions.

Singing to your plants can have similar stimulating effects. Traditional American Hopi Indian farmers have long done so. Sessions of drumming in the Men of the Trees plant nursery in Perth gave the most enhanced plant growth in experiments conducted there.

T.C.N. Singh studied the effects of music and dance on plant growth at the Bihar Agricultural College in India. It was found that Indian ragas and dancing (presumably Indian dance) near plants improved their health and growth levels. [2]

Love those plants

As plants respond to our thoughts, feelings and intentions it behoves us to think of them lovingly, and to converse with them as necessary, whether mentally or verbally, in order to develop a co-creative synergy between us. Say sorry before culling and give plants plenty of warning of your intentions before pruning or transplanting them. To also reduce shock at such times - water them with a few drops of added flower essence Rescue Remedy. 'Laying on of hands' is a useful healing technique too. By resonating with love amongst your plants, gardening can be truly soul satisfying work.

References:

1 - 'A Dowser's Model', T. E. Ross, ASD Journal, vol 23, no 2, May 1983.
2 - Bihar Agricultural College magazine, vol.13, no. 1.

2.4 Stones in the Garden

Makin gardens grow!

Gerald Makin of Tasmania, was getting nowhere with gardening. He discovered dowsing and read with great interest about ancient megalith cultures. He learned that the inhospitable high land of Dartmoor, in the English county of Devon, had once grown substantial food crops and supported a sizable population. There are standing stones running in rows or found singly all across Dartmoor.

Dowsing indicated to Makin that it would be possible to enhance soil fertility by placing a standing stone in the garden. By dowsing he determined that a stone he had would fit the bill. He dowsed a position for the stone on a garden plan, as well as its depth and orientation, then set it up. He then detected an energy line going from his stone to a neighbouring garden, where an elderly Cornish woman friend also had a standing stone. (She was versed in ancient Cornish secret wisdom - of geomancy, cosmology and magic, and is now deceased.)

Things didn't start moving, however, until other stones were erected and energy lines criss-crossed the half acre garden. By then the original stone also radiated about 30 energy lines, while an energy spiral / Earth vortex that had formed around it filled the whole garden. Beside each garden bed he placed a small stone, over 30 in all, to carry and transmit Earth ch'i (energy). Makin's garden from then on began to flourish.

Megaliths and Miniliths

Into recent times crop failure in quiet corners of rural Britain has been blamed on the prior removal or destruction of local standing stones and stone circles in the area. It is felt that the ancestors did their extensive 'megalithic engineering' works to ensure agricultural harmony. The belief in the fertilising powers of stone still lives on strongly. A resurgance of interest in geomantic wisdom has inspired many people, like Makin, to emulate the old ways.

Some people place stone pillars on the north and south ends of garden beds to stimulate natural energy flows and enhance soil fertility. Circles of stones, specially selected by dowsing (or intuition) for the purpose, are placed around a sick plant for vitalising and healing.

American dowser Harvey Lisle created over one hundred small stone circles on his farm and enjoys high productivity from it. The stone circles, he finds, emit low-energy lines which criss cross the garden between them. He uses paramagnetic stone, with usually 8 rocks around each tree, and these are aligned to the directions with a compass.

He has also placed 12 stones around a strong Earth energy point, where 2 ley lines cross, to act as a stone Medicine Wheel, of American Indian tradition. From there he controls a number of functions on the farm. Lisle, whose farm is featured in the book 'Secrets of the Soil', recommends placing a stone circle wherever there's a special energy place. He previously had problems raising young fruit trees, but after starting to use the stone circles, trees began to flourish. [1]

The physical benefits of stone mulching of plants have been expounded by J.I. Rodale, the famous US organic growing pioneer, who published a book 'Stone Mulching in the Garden' in 1949. Stone mulch, he says, allows micro organisms and other soil fauna the freedom to operate without disturbance; it conserves water, allows for good soil aeration, improves mycorrhizal root associations, helps regulate temperatures and provides some break-down nutrients.[2] It also prevents chickens from scratching, and stones don't blow away in the wind or burn in bushfires, as paper or straw mulch do very easily.

Mounds

Garden berms and mounds are good at accumulating Earth ch'i and also help rainwater to penetrate the soil. Ellen V. Wilmont Ware wrote, in 1953, about a method of land rehabilitation that she devised using special garden mounds.

Starting with a circular saucer-like depression dug in the ground, with a few stones placed in the centre, she piles a mound of Earth and humus on top and plants into it. Rainfall is driven by air pressure towards the core of the mound, thence spiralling downwards into the Earth to naturally replenish groundwater, she says. [3]

Other dowsers have found that a mound with spiralling stones around it -

called a 'herb spiral', can generate a subtle energy vortex around it for some distance. If the stones are paramagnetic, this is not at all surprising.

Given the insights of 'stone-age farming'- rock gardening takes on a whole new significance.

References:

1 - Secrets of the Soil, C. Bird & P. Tompkins, Harpers and Row, 1989.
2 - 'Stone Mulching in the Garden' J. Rodale, Rodale Institute, USA, 1949.
3 - 'Pendulum' magazine, UK, Ellen V. Wilmont Ware, 1953.

2.5 Psycho-spiritual techniques

Plants and prayer

Researching the effect of mind over matter, Rev Franklin Loer, director of the Religious Research Foundation of Los Angeles, experimented with the power of prayer on water used on test plants. The plants watered with the blessed water prospered far above the controls. In another test, reported in his book 'The Power of Prayer on Plants' 150 people visualised 27,000 seeds to be thriving under ideal conditions of growth. This accelerated their growth rate by up to 20%.

Dr Robert Miller, an industrial research scientist and former professor of chemical engineering at Georgia Technical College, USA, showed that this factor was operative at a great distance. In 1967 he measured a greatly increased growth rate in plants after a healer tuned into them briefly from 600 kms away. For those who wish to try blessing plants, bless seeds and soil before planting, and then daily after watering.

The Magnetron

The magnetron is a symbolic pattern for radionic type work, that helps to transmit thoughts to plants. A witness (soil, plant sample etc) is placed on the manetron, together with suitable remedies or soil amendments, in the form of witnesses, or just the names written on paper. A pendulum is rotated over the diagram for the dowsed amount of time (or until it stops rotating) and number of treatment sessions.

One magnetron experiment described by Christopher Hill, in 'The Electro-Vibratory Body', involved an organic vegetable garden with a history of pest invasion. This garden was divided into nine plots separated by pathways. It was decided to try to clear sowbugs from the worst affected plot, so a piece of soil and a live bug from the chosen plot were placed in the centre of the magnetron.

The bug was then killed to broadcast its death vibrations to the plot and left undisturbed for 2 weeks. Within 3 days of doing this there was not a trace of the sow bugs in that particular plot and they didn't return all summer. Meanwhile, in the control plots, normal sow bug activity continued as usual.

When transferring thoughts to the garden stick to one idea at a time and keep visualisations simple. Be fair, allowing insect predators something to eat, and work with a spirit of unconditional love. You can also send love to the garden via a crystal on a garden photo witness that's placed on the magnetron (seen below). [1]

The magnetron

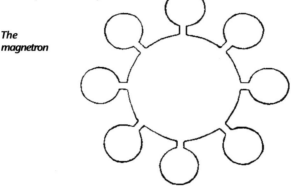

Circle and arrow

The circle and arrow is a radionic type pattern used in pest control. NSW dowser Isabel Bellamy reported how a farmer, tired of losing so much fruit to the rosella parrots, tried the following method.

Finding the dead body of a rosella he drew a big circle on cardboard with the numbers 1 to 100 marked around it and oriented it to north. He dowsed over this circle to find the direction of origin of the parrots.

He then drew a second circle inside the first with an arrow from the centre pointing in the birds' direction. Then he put the dead rosella in the centre of that circle.

Although the birds returned the next day, when they arrived there was a great commotion amongst them and they soon headed off. After this happened 3 times they stopped coming altogether.

Birds vs Birds

Other people have had success with the circle and arrow method, but it doesn't always work. It is a good idea to seek out practical solutions to problems first. A permaculture method, which simply uses nature, is to set up a dovecot of pigeons in the orchard. Pigeons are very territorial birds, as Graeme Nalder, president of the Murray-Mallee Organic Growers group, found out when he tried this. And they only eat grain. Previously he had lost 80-90% of fruit in his house orchard, but with the pigeons keeping intruders away this loss dropped to a mere 10%. [2]

Thought - form fence

American dowser Fred Kantor described how to construct a mental force field barrier around one's garden in an ASD journal. Fred's garden was plagued by all sorts of predators so he decided to try out a 'thought-form fence'. His dowsing told him that it would work so, with his L-rods, he queried the size, depth, location and other details - building up the power of the thought form as he went along.

He then ripped down the ineffective electric fence around the garden, rototilled and planted as usual. Despite his family's scepticism the resulting garden grew perfectly well without predation, despite plenty of animals browsing in the vicinity. Fred then went on to successfully build a thought - form fence remotely for a friend 100 miles distant, and was in demand to build others afterwards.

Once again, this technique, cannot always be guaranteed, and depends on the operator!

Working with devas

Giant cabbages and minimal pest predation are the hallmarks of famous gardens at Findhorn (Scotland) and Perelandra (USA)- shining examples of productive working relationships between gardeners and the spirits of nature.

These amazing gardens were achieved by opening lines of communication with the archetypal consciousness of the devas - the overlighting spirits of plants, animals and gardens, and gaining their advice. At Findhorn this was in the form of straightforward meditation by experienced psychics. At the Perelandra garden Machaelle Wright Small uses a form of muscle testing (equivalent to body dowsing), to gain access to devic levels of consciousness.

Machaelle suggests that initially one can say aloud: "I wish to be formally linked with the devic realm." As contact is made one might then feel sensations, like waves of energy gently washing over you. With a divining tool, she then asks for devic guidance in garden design, advice on what to plant and where, and how to best deal with insects. To control insect pests she offers to tithe a certain part of her crop to them. This keeps the garden, the pests and the pest's predators happy.

Machaelle's method of fertilising the garden also involves the devas. She makes up a 'soil balancing kit' of various organic substances suggested by the devas. The collection comprises small packages of bone meal, rock phosphate, cottonseed meal, (paramagnetic) greensand, dolomite, lime, kelp and comfrey. She takes a pinch of each substance individually and holds it in the palm of her hand, asking the appropriate devas what amount is needed. She then asks that they receive the energy of that nutrient and take the right amount down to the right soil depth where it's needed in the garden. After about 10 seconds the transfer is completed, sensed as a change in the nutrient, or sensation in the hand, and the sample thrown away.

Machaelle's garden has an incredible rate of production and is never watered, even during drought, except at planting time. The devas, she says,
"seek a co-creative partnership with humans
and they are in the position to accept no less." [3]

Pranic farming

Originating in India, pranic farming techniques aim to heal the land and impart beneficial energies to it for improved crop growth. The system involves colour therapy treatments, broadcasting different colours at different growth phases, such as red light for faster germination, as well as specific treatments for cases of disease or infestation. Pranic cultivation methods, such as chanting in the fields and other ancient techniques of pranic fertilising are also undertaken.

To quote a leaflet from the Pranic Healing School: Pranic Psychotherapy is used for land which has undergone violations and involves psychically broadcasting electric violet, ordinary violet or white. In cleansing the

81

land one includes a 3-10m (10–30') radius around the targetted field, using the following colour spectrum- light to medium green; and then light orange (which helps the Earth to better absorb nutrients and prana).

Citrine crystals are planted in the 4 corners or around the field, having been programmed for continuous cleansing and absorption of negative elements. A master crystal can be used at home for monitoring.

Meditation on 'Twin Hearts', 'Masters Om' or 'Om Shanti' can be played to complete the cleansing. Special invocations are made to the devas, angels, nature spirits and Mother Earth for one's intention, especially for continuous presence and blessings.

Energising work is pratised, including energising the soil supplements. Light to medium red is sent to the soil. After seeds are planted they are energised with electric violet. For the preceeding days they are energised with red/red-yellow/violet.

When seeds have germinated, one stops the colours and leaves the work to Mother Nature, the Sun and the angels/devas. Meditation on 'Twin Hearts', 'Om' or 'Om Shanti' is played several times in the field. The number of healing sessions depends on the crop.

"Familiarity, respect, gratitude and harmony with Mother Earth, the angels/devas of nature and the nature spirits", they say, "will build the synergy among the workers (inner and outer) in the field". [4]

References:

1 - 'The Electro-Vibratory Body', Christopher Hills,
University of the Trees, USA.
2 - 'Hot Permaculture Tips', Alanna Moore, Green Connections, Dec 2000.
3 - 'The Perelandra Garden Workbook, a complete guide to working
with nature intelligences,'
Machaelle W. Small, PO Box 136 Jeffersonton, Virginia 22724, USA.
4 - Natural Resonance Study Group newsletter, Dec. 2000, Perth WA.
Pranic Healing School Institute of Inner Studies, Western Australia,
phone 08 9388 6151.

2.6 *Agricultural Coils*

Copper

Copper is a great conductor of subtle energies and copper wire is often the preferred material for making Earth healing and energy balancing devices, such as agricultural radiesthetic coils. It has also been found that stringing a copper wire 'antenna', oriented north - south, above a row of plants will attract and focus energy onto a crop and enhance production.

Copper is also the best metal for soil cultivation tools, as it will not disrupt natural Earth energy flows, Austrian 'water wizard' Victor Shauberger discovered. Schauberger had been invited to go to Bulgaria to check out the problem of farmland soils drying out.

The Bulgarians were using steam ploughs of steel, but in old Turkish settlements wooden ploughs were still in use and the soil there was not drying out. Thinking the plough must be the problem he experimented with copper coated plough shares.

Shauberger had deduced that steel and iron have a detrimental effect on the water characteristics within the soil, as Earth's magnetism gets cut and diverged by such modern farm implements. Also, tiny particles of steel which grind off machinery cause oxidation and rust, depriving the soil of oxygen, killing certain microorganisms and causing groundwater to sink, thus drying out the land. Ploughs of wood, copper and other 'biologically magnetic' materials don't disturb the Earth's magnetic field, he decided.

Shauberger reaped a 50% bigger harvest of high quality crop with his copper plated plough shares. In 1950 Shauberger and engineer Rosenberger patented a method of coating active surfaces of farm machinery with copper. He also invented a spiral plough which directed soil in a centripetal motion, just as a mole would dig the soil.

Today, tools of copper and beryllium are manufactured by a large technical company in Germany for use in private homes and nurseries. They're not as hard as steel, and when they deteriorate beneficial trace minerals are put into the soil, increasing bio-electrical potential. [1]

Many dowsers have brought harmony to farmland or crops by installing special metal loops and coils. These coils may well be functioning as modern equivalents of standing stones, attracting cosmic or Earth rays necessary for soil health. No-one really knows the mechanism at work, but the empirical evidence suggests they can be a simple means of enhancing agriculture (although not everyone has success with them).

Lakhovsky / French coil

The observation that all living cells emit radio signals and generate weak electrical fields revealed an important potential for healing to research physicist Dr Herbert Pohl, director of the Pohl Cancer Research Laboratory in Oklahoma. In 1985 Pohl reported his discovery that electrically sensitive powders are pulled through a cell as if by a magnet, whilst their non-electrical counterparts are not. The radio emissions amplified during cell division may play a role in function, growth and healing, he suspected, so Pohl suggested that if frequencies could be controlled so too could the development of cancer.

Pohl's ideas were not new, they echoed the largely forgotten research of Georges Lakhovsky, a Russian born engineer resident in Paris until the 1930's. Lakhovsky

Lakhosky oscillator

was also the first person to experiment with high frequency electromagnetic waves in biology, paving the way for the first International Congress of Radiobiology, held in Venice in 1934. His theories became popular in Europe with the publication in 1939 of 'The Secret of Life - Cosmic Rays and Radiations of Living Beings', now out of print. It was unfortunate timing, with Europe in turmoil, and consequently his work did not receive the recognition it deserved. Lakhovsky's new science of radiobiology bridged physics, biology and medicine, and it antagonised orthodox medical practitioners.

As with Pohl, cellular radiation was the basis of Lakhovsky's discoveries.

He compared the nucleus of a living cell to an electrical oscillating circuit, due to the presence of tubular twisted filament - the chromosomes - being surrounded by conducting fluid. This endows qualities of capacity and inductance, and the ability to oscillate to a specific frequency. The cell thus resembles a radio receiver, with its coils and circuits. It is able to transmit or receive very short radio-electric waves, and give rise to high frequency currents in the nuclear circuitry which are maintained by the energy of the cosmic rays. In this light, oscillatory disequilibrium may be seen as a precursor to disease, and the regularisation of the cosmic field as a key to healing.

In 1923 Lakhovsky's invention - the radiocellulo-oscillator - was used successfully to treat and cure geraniums inoculated with cancer, by utilising ultra-short Hertzian waves. A second series of experiments using an oscillating circuit, a loop without artificial excitation, proved equally successful. This circuit, Lakhovsky explained, created a resonance between the constant field of atmospheric cosmic waves necessary for local harmonisation. The restored cellular oscillations would then impart more regularised cell division, greater immunity and resistance to disease, plus the ability to withstand insect attack. Circuits were eagerly applied to patients in many European and American hospitals and nursing homes, as well as to plants and animals.

The empirical value of Lakhovsky's inventions, supported by astonishing photographs of regenerated tissue in plants and animals, gradually silenced the hostile critics and skeptics around him. A prominent anti-Nazi, Lakhovsky fled to New York where he died in 1942, aged 73.

Lakhovsky coils are very easy to make and use. Simply cut a suitable length of wire, preferably copper, and loop it once, with the ends left slightly apart. Ascertain, with the pendulum, the polarity of each end. Then site it horizontally around a sick plant, positioning the negative pole uppermost and checking each step with the pendulum. Keep the loop in place with string or wooden supports, then wait and see what happens. American dowsers speak of positioning these coils within the 'front door' of the plant. Results may take a year or more to become apparent in large trees.

Marie Neil, an historian and dowser from Castle Hill, Sydney, wrote to me of her success with the French coil. *"Two large gum trees which grew directly over an underground stream had suffered bad insect infestation and were dying,"* she said. *"The (Earth acupuncture) stakes had been placed in position too late to save them. We saved them, however, by placing Lakhovsky oscillators around their trunks."*

"We dowsed the number of oscillators required for each tree, the size of the gap to be left in the ring, the distance up the trunk at which to nail the oscillators in position and the distance between the oscillators when two were required on one tree."

"These oscillators were simply open ended rings made of wire similar to coat hanger wire, which had been purchased from a hardware store. Dowsing also indicated the length of time the oscillators were to stay in position. New healthy growth soon appeared. Today both trees are strong and completely healthy."

Frank Moody, mid 1980's
photo - Steven Guth.

Moody Coil

Frank Moody, a 97 year old geomancer from Queensland, has improved upon the Lakhovsky Coil by extending each end, to become an antenna and Earth wire, and attaching these vertical components onto a wooden stake. He uses these coils for plant healing, neutralising georadiations and uplifting farm production generally. For the latter effect Moody positions coils halfway along boundary lines, often 2m (8') up to escape horses, or 2 on opposite boundary sides, facing in to each other.

In the northern hemisphere Frank winds the loop clockwise, in the southern hemisphere - anti-clockwise. He uses copper, galvanised or aluminium wire. Coil diameter, with up to 3.5m (11') being trialled, and antenna size is governed by the size of the area under treatment. The gap between the base of the antenna and earth ends must be small, however, at 5-10mm (quarter to half inch), and the Earth wire must penetrate the ground at least 15cm (6"). While small versions are self-supporting, larger coils need timber supports. The influence of these coils, he says, radiates sideways and forwards of the vertical antenna.

Marie Neil successfully used a Moody coil for sickly plants, reporting *"I don't use specific measurements for the gap and it doesn't seem to matter."*

Seven turn coil

Lakhovsky developed a variation of his one turn coil which he used specifically for trees. He measured the girth of the tree 60cm (2') up the trunk, then multiplied this figure by eight. A length of insulated copper wire (single flex electrical) was then cut.

Next he ascertained the polarity of each end by dowsing, tying a knot in the negative end. This knot was tacked over the point of the 'front door' and the wire wound seven times up the tree, each coil being about 25mm (1") apart. The top positive end was then tacked down to the trunk.

A similar type of coil is made in this way. Walk around a sick tree whilst dowsing to find the 'front door'. One end of a length of copper wire is thrust into the ground to a depth of 10-15cm (4"- 6") in front of this 'door' and is then looped several times up the trunk. The other end of the wire is bent skywards.

The coil is kept in position for 18 months. You need to check occasionally if the position remains correct in relation to the 'front door'.

Nine turn coil

Clive Hull, a new age agricultural researcher in New Zealand, wrote about his own coil.

"In the garden a 9 turn right hand coil made a 25% increase in the growth of sunflowers. It was the seed head that made the real improvement.

The coil didn't surround the sunflower and was made from copper wire welded onto a 10cm (4") nail."

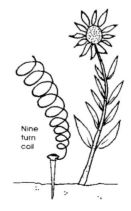

Nine turn coil

Vertical spiral

Also known as a Holdingyard or kite coil, this device had its earliest known use by the late Mrs Muriel Harrison, a dynamic dowser, radionics practitioner and teacher from Adelaide, South Australia. She used pairs of these spirals (from 2 to 15) to create positive, neutral or negative resonating fields for the garden.

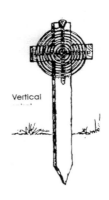

Vertical

One spiral of each pair is wound clockwise from the centre, the other is wound anti-clockwise. With the pendulum the number of spirals is determined, plus their best compass point positions.

Vertical spiral coil

To construct such a spiral - use wire that has been selected by dowsing for the appropriate metal and gauge, and attach it to a board or wooden cross at a predetermined height. Keep the coils in place with copper ribbon or tacks. Start coiling from the centre, where 3cm (1") of wire is left pointing out at right angles. Dowse the distance between each turn. Isabel Bellamy suggests using a solid pyramid shape as a spiral former.

With clockwise spirals, the central end must dowse as negative. Onto this end you can solder a small metal funnel for holding witnesses of healing agents, to act as a radionic remedy broadcaster. Suitable substances are found by dowsing. If samples are not available, try writing their names on paper and inserting them into the funnel.

Vertical coil
photo-Steven Guth

Another method, using colour healing, is to place bundles of suitably coloured embroidery threads into the funnel. To ascertain which colours, dowse over a colour chart together with a soil witness for 'colour hunger'. Measure out suitable lengths of the thread with the pendulum, then knot them together and use.

Frank Moody has modified this coil also. His vertical spiral coil has a diameter of about 1m (1yd) with about 8 to 14 turns of wire stapled on a vertical wooden cross.

The un-earthed positive end is in the centre and the coils go clockwise in the southern hemisphere. On the outer negative end, a little copper witness box is soldered with the colour orange, represented by embroidery thread, found to be generally useful. This spiral can be earthed, in which case wind the coils the opposite way. Energy is said to project forwards from this coil.

Frank has used his coils to rid farms of rabbits, in which case they are coiled with the central end negative in an anti clockwise direction and the positive end earthed. To the central end is attached a copper tube containing colour witnesses, plugged to keep rain out.

For rabbits, a combination of red and green using two whole cotton skeins has proved effective. The energy circulates along the lie of the land, but won't lift above 3.5m (10'), so it's useless for troublesome lorikeets in fruit trees. Moody reports 90% success on 2 farms in northern Tasmania and that *"a side effect not anticipated is the uncharacteristic behaviour of wallabies."*

Other coils

Tasmanian Ross Henderson's farm was in bad shape when he acquired it. Inspired by dowsing mentor Ralph Thomas's 'radiesthetic coils' he invented his own brand of agricultural 'radiator' coil, using galvanised, copper or fencing wire, designed by dowsing and placed on energy points in the landscape. Since then Ross has virtually no need for fertilisers, his cattle stocking rate is up and he has no calving problems. Just too many rabbits!

US dowser Verne Cameron uses coils and cones for energy balancing in the environment. Flat coils, he finds, placed horizontally, emit a force upward and downward. Energy quality changes when coils are flipped over.

Other people use pyramids to stimulate seed germination, speed up growth and generally improve crops. The spiral vortex, cone and pyramid forms have always been considered sacred or special, and are energetically similar. The 'dunce's cap' of old probably works on this principle, stimulating mental processes in slow learners.

References:

1 - 'Living Water - Victor Schauberger and the Secrets of Natural Energy', Olof Alexandersson, Turnstone Press, 1982.

PART THREE: DYNAMIC GROWING

Modern Biodynamics

Biodynamics, a well established system of eco-farming from the Germanic tradition, was founded by Rudolph Steiner, who gave his famous series of agriculture lectures in 1924. Steiner was clairvoyant and also a keen observer of ancient folk traditions on farms. His system of farming may be regarded as overly esoteric to the average farmer, yet scientific research has been backing up many of the principles involved.

Steiner advocated that farmers and gardeners stimulate both the Earthly and atmospheric forces of the land, and called for a 'lively interchange taking place between what is above ground and what is below'. Thus biodynamic techniques are practised in accordance with the appropriate times of lunar, solar and planetary activity for best results. Planting is always best done according to moon and sun phases. (While this is fine in Europe, however, in Australia's dry climate it is often better to plant according to when it rains!)

Steiner devised recipes, with fermented, potentised sprays made from cow manure, crushed crystal and various herbs. In modern terms this was providing microbial inoculation and as well as homoeopathic effects, which trigger life processes to flourish and multiply.

The most important biodynamic recipe for soil fertility calls for cow horns full of healthy cow manure to be buried at a certain moon phase and left underground over the course of winter. Potent Earth energies at that time of year help it to transform into a microbe rich substance, called '500'. When it is dug up in spring the manure has become an odourless substance of deep green colour, which is as close to pure humus as anything, and when applied to soil is a fabulous soil activator. (It is usual to mix a tiny amount of 500 into the manure before stuffing if into horns, to inoculate it with microbes.)

A small amount of this material is stirred in water for exactly one hour in a particular way. The water is stirred for 19 or 20 seconds in a clockwise direction, creating a deep vortex; then the vortex is reversed by stirring anti-clockwise for 19 or 20 seconds. When changing directions a raging chaos is created for 4 or 5 seconds. After the hour of stirring, the resulting liquid is then sprayed onto the land in a specific manner at a specific time, when the ground is damp. Several generations of biodynamic farmers can now attest to the value of carrying out Steiner's suggestions. Topsoil can be quickly rebuilt with 500 plus good farming practise.

In transferring the European ideas of Steiner to Australia there has been much research and experimentation to find the best suited practices, as Steiner would have wanted happen. Our soils are much older, more leached and the climate is much drier. So adaptations are inevitable, and may upset the purists.

BD meets geomancy

Some people, writes Hugh Lovel, have looked at enhancing 500 production by burying the horns where there are junctions of Earth energy lines, or within stone circles. He suggests that horns be arranged in a vortex pattern in the ground, with horn tips placed point upwards. [2]

Clay remedy

Steiner was probably familiar with an ancient German farming technique called 'clay singing', as observed by Victor Shauberger. Shauberger described a visit, in the high Bavarian forest country, to an eccentric old farmer who always had the best harvests in the area. It was nearly evening and the farmer was stirring a wooden barrel of water with a large wooden spoon. As he stirred he chanted a musical scale loudly down into the barrel, pitched at a certain resonance level and not always pleasant to hear. As he sang up the scale he stirred in an anti-clockwise direction, then his voice deepened as he changed direction and sang down the scale. Occasionally the farmer flicked some loamy clay soil into the barrel.

The farmer then muttered that it was ready to 'ferment'. Early the next morning the barrel was taken out into the fields and, with a strong palm tree frond in hand, the farmer sprinkled the water over the freshly rolled fields. 'Tonsingen' was once a common practice, done only at specific

91

Stirring up Life

Lyn West lives in a biodynamic oasis on a suburban house block in Queanbeyan, southern NSW. Lyn's secrets of lush growth include moon planting, biodynamic compost and an unique fermented liquid seaweed fertiliser, both of which Lyn makes on-site.

Lyn was stirring a big tank of murky liquid as she explained to me what went into her commercial seaweed product and what made it so special. "Most liquid manures are anaerobic. This one is aerobic." She went on to explain how the liquid is gently pumped through a series of Virbela flowforms twice weekly to energise it, while oxygenating pumps are employed in the tanks for a couple of hours daily. Six bags of BD preps were dangling in the brew.

It takes 5 months for the added microbial culture to break down and liquify the seaweed which Lyn collects under license from Ulladulla.

The presence of this aerobic bacteria is highly beneficial for humus production in soils. She now has biodynamic certification for her 'BioActive' seaweed, from the Biological Farmers Association.

Lyn studied biodynamics with Alex Podolinsky, Terry Foreman and Brian Keats. She developed a real passion for the subject and began to give talks to various groups to spread the word. In 1996 she trained as a field advisor for the BFA and is now their regional field advisor.

But part-time employment, necessary to help raise 2 kids on her own, took up much of her time and energy. Finally she made the bold move to drop her job and focus fully on biodynamics. She had spent months writing a study course in biodynamics which she wanted to teach.

"I couldn't go on not expressing my need to practise biodynamics fully. It was deadening me not to."

When she decided to follow her true calling she got the green light. Hoping that at least 10 people would enrol for the course she went ahead and advertised it. She had to close the books after 30 people had enrolled!

Contact Lynette West, Universal Biological Solutions, 30 McIntosh St, Queanbeyan 2620, ph 02 6297 2729, fax 02 6299 2440.

Right: Flowforms keep the liquid fertiliser aerobic.

times, such as after planting and firming of the seed, at around Easter time. By the early 20th century the custom was already subject to ridicule and dying out.

Shauberger felt that the spraying of the clay water onto soil was providing a film or filter between the positively charged atmosphere and negative Earth which "attracted rays from all directions and then gave them out again." [1]

Horn clay

Hugh Lovel has been developing biodynamic agricultural methods on his farm in the USA and writes about his work in 'Acres USA'. Lovel has lately been enthusing about the new BD prep – horn clay. Apparently Steiner had promised during his famous agricultural seminars that he would explain about a remedy for clay, but it was never forthcoming. He got sick after giving the first lot of lectures and was dead within six months.

The clay remedy is now being developed in the US. Horn clay is meant to mediate between the two main BD sprays 500 and 501, as Steiner had suggested, and I imagine it may be supplying traces of essential minerals not found in those preparations.

"Horn manure (500) enlivens soil, while horn silica (501) enlivens the atmosphere" writes Hugh Lovel "and with horn clay everything is brought together and integrated. Horn clay is a must on sandy, rocky soils, but it works even better on heavy clays. It really wakes things up and they grow very well indeed."

Originally Steiner said to fill the open ends of the cow horns, after stuffing them with manure and silica, with a plug of clay. But he never explained why, just hinted that more would be revealed in a second series of lectures that never eventuated. Nowadays people are filling whole horns with clay (which may be paramagnetic) and these are buried for a full year, from spring to spring, or autumn to autumn. Alternatively- a clay plug is added to the top of the 500 and 501 horns, which are dug up in summer and winter for mixed application. Only a small handful to the hectare (rounded tablespoon to the acre) is needed for spraying on the soil, as compared to a double handful of 500 or 2 pinches of 501 to the hectare (a handful 500 or a pinch of 501 to the acre). The use of horn clay has only recently been taken up, but results are very worthwhile, Hugh has written. [1]

The Biodynamic Farmers and Gardeners Association of Australia are currently experimenting with making and using horn clay, at their north Dorrigo, NSW, major preparation making site. They have also started to make horn basalt dust, it was reported in summer 2001. [3]

BD Pest Control

BD pest control is undertaken according to specific cosmic influences and is known as 'peppering'. A couple of handfuls of weed seeds are burnt at the appropriate time with wood then ground fine in a mortar and pestle (but leave out the wood ash, or you may devitalise trees!). This can be put in a pepper shaker and sprinkled on affected ground, wherever those weeds are prevalent. Lovel suggests that better results are had from a field spray of a homeopathic 7x or 8x potency, which is either sprayed or broadcast radionically. Results may take 2 to 3 years.

To deter insect pests, bugs are also collected and burnt to ash, and this is best done when the Sun is in Taurus. For adult insects the Aries side of Taurus and for young insects the Gemini side of Taurus are the best times to act. Otherwise you can simply blend the insects in a blender and spray them around when needed.

For animals pests, such as rabbits, Steiner recommended burning the hide of the animal during the high conjunction of Venus with Scorpio. The next best time, says Lovel, is when Venus is in Scorpio, especially when Venus is on the far side of the Sun from the Earth. These times are few and far between, so Lovel does it whenever Venus is in Scorpio and ashes the skin, grinds the ashes and makes a homoeopeopathic potency from it to spray or radionically broadcast around affected areas. [2]

The modern biodynamic researcher can greatly benefit by dowsing to determine how appropriate certain methods or remedies may be for their own unique situation. Then we could say that this form of agriculture is being truly dynamic, and not slavishly adhering to sets of rules that were formulated by Steiner long before the modern era had fully changed the nature of farming, and technology had imposed its own problematic regime.

BD in OZ not always OK

"Is Biodynamics appropriate in Australia?" wrote Anthony Riddell of Collingwood, in Geomantica magazine. "In 1996 I studied bio-dynamic farming and gardening, but that body of knowledge strikes me as overtly Euro-centric. I have posited 'Indigenous Bio-dynamics' (IBD) or 'Biodynamic Bush-Tucker' - something along those lines. Is this energetically possible?"

Steven Guth was having similar thoughts, when he wrote a piece about using 500 in an Australian landscape. A friend of his had given some to him and organized for it to be spread around the house, by being flicked out with a small brush. Over the next 2 days a blue haze gathered over the lawn.

On the third day Steven woke up and, unusually, there was not a bird to be heard around the house. That day he was deeply depressed. Checking later, he found that 2 others in the household had days of depression that started that morning.

He thinks that the 500 somehow clashed with the Australian devas, and that, as a caretaker he had goofed! The European grasses in the lawn, meanwhile, were growing exceptionally well! [3]

Biodynamic farmer Barbara Hedley has also addressed this question. She has pointed out that just because BD practises work well on European crops, this doesn't mean that all vegetation benefits. The needs and energies of Australian native vegetation are very different from our cultivated plants.

She believes that remnants of native vegetation should be excluded from stock and allowed to be what she calls 'deva stations' - left undisturbed, like the sacred groves of old, to be the home of the nature spirits. Areas of wilderness don't appreciate the BD sprays, and farmers are best to avoid spraying any preps, or radionically broadcasting them to these areas, Barbara says. [3]

BD and rainfall

What have Towers of Power, Agnihotra and biodynamics got in common? They all claim to be able to make it rain!

It was the American energy researcher Wilhelm Reich who made the observation that times of drought were always accompanied by sluggish atmospheric conditions, with atmospheric ether congested with DOR – deadly orgone radiation, as he called it. (Feng shui people might call it 'sh'a' or simply 'bad energy').

Reich conducted a great deal of research in the early 1950's on how to clear toxic atmospheric conditions. He lived downwind from nuclear testing sites, so there was plenty of DOR around. His 'cloudbuster' (a series of pipes pointed skywards and connected to running water on the ground) was used to suck atmospheric energy around the sky and to make it rain, but it is a rather dangerous device.

Hugh Lovel and Hugh Courtney have recently devised a gentler technique of atmospheric energy balancing and clearing, which involves spraying BD preps in a particular sequence over several days. In 4 days it will rain, they say! (This definately needs to be tested in Australia!)

The sequence is to spray 500, then 501, then barrel compost*, 508, and 500 again. Whenever hazy dry conditions have set in, Lovel repeats this sequence, always with success, except once when Mercury was retrograde.

Courtney does it usually 2 or 3 days before full moon, when it tends to rain more, and ideally when the moon is in a water constellation. Lovel begins by spraying barrel compost onto soil at sunset and sunrise, accompanied by a light spray of horsetail for balance (the herb horsetail/equistifolia has high silica content).

Lovel claims to have made it rain across a 32km (20 mile) to 160km (100 mile) radius area with this technique.

These days Lovel uses the easier method of broadcasting the BD preps radionically. Using a Malcolm Rae radionics machine he does morning and evening broadcasts of the same sequence, using an aerial photo as a witness and homoeopathic potencies of the BD preps. [2]

* **Barrel compost** is a special BD compost, made from pure cow manure that has been composted in a barrel buried in the ground. The manure heap has 6 BD preps inserted into it.

The recipe devised by Maria Thun is even better - cow manure, ground egg shells (from healthy organically raised hens) and basalt dust are combined with the preps 502 – 507 and left for 12 weeks. One barrelful is enough to spray onto 880 hectares (2000 acres). It makes a very good pioneering spray, when converting to biodynamic methods, she says. [5]

References:

1- 'Living Water - Victor Schauberger and the Secrets of Natural Energy', Olof Alexanderson, Turnstone Press, 1982.
2- 'Agricultural Renewal- A Basis for Social Change', Hugh Lovel, 2000, Union Agriculture Institute, 8475 Dockery Rd, Blairsville, Georgia 30512, USA. Email - uai@alltel.net
3- 'Geomantica', no 6, summer 1999.
4- 'Newsleaf', Journal of the Biodynamic Farming and Gardening Association, summer 2000, PO Box 54 Bellingen, 2454, Australia. Email - bdoffice@biodynamics.net.au
5- 'Secrets of the Soil', C. Bird and P. Tompkins, Harper and Row,1989.

3:2 Earth Spirited Permaculture

Many people these days are adopting an ethic of Earth-care in order to help halt environmental destruction. They realise that it is their own consumption patterns that are part of the problem. There's a growing respect for the preciousness of life on Earth, her diversity and magic. Permaculture offers solutions to many environmental problems and can provide hope, inspiration and empowerment. This design concept was created by Australians Bill Mollison and David Holmgren over 20 years ago.

Why Permaculture?

Permaculture is a way of saving the planet by starting in your own backyard. It's a design system which aims to create productive human environments that provide food, shelter, energy and other needs. When you eat your own organically produced food you raise the energy resonance levels of your local environment and yourself, as well as save on money, greenhouse gases from transportation etc.

By not supporting unsustainable agriculture your consumer power sends strong messages to the economic system that subsidises it, for the benefit of multinational corporate profits alone.

Aims and ethics

Modelled on nature, permaculture systems (permanent cultures) aim for sustainability, by having the biodiversity, stability and resilience of natural ecosystems. From agriculture to human lifestyle and culture - permaculture has practical answers to local and global problems.

The ethics of permaculture are to care for the Earth and people, and to contribute surplus time, money and energy to achieve these ends. Underlying this lies the basic life ethic which recognises the intrinsic worth of every living thing. Working in harmony and cooperation with nature is the permaculture way.

There is an emphasis on connectedness and co-operative lifestyles in permaculture, which challenges the dominant paradigm of competitive individualism. Steering society away from our current path of destruction requires a pardigm shift back to old ways of knowing, feeling and sensing, and to holistic values irrelevant to the economic system.

Food for the Soul

Permaculture combines wisdom contained in traditional farming systems with modern scientific and appropriate technological advances. Permaculture planning integrates the inherent qualities of plants and animals with the natural characteristics of landscapes and structures, in order to create healthy, sustainable production systems for both city and country. Principles of geomancy, feng shui and paganism complement permaculture principles beautifully. We can listen to the land and let it speak for itself, honour its capability and heed its limitations.

We can create landscapes of harmony, beauty and productivity, and reduce negative impacts on the planet. It starts with our attitude and it nourishes not only our bodies and minds, but our hearts and spirits too.

Ch'i energy

Stable ecologies thrive on biological diversity, on networks of plant and animal cultures (called 'guilds' in permaculture) in energetic relationship. Such healthy, diverse environments produce surpluses for us to eat with few pest problems to worry about.

Energy storage is a primary aim of permaculture design. All forms of natural energies are collected, stored and used on-site (or sold back to the electricity grid!). For example: we can plant windbreaks and sun traps to retain winter warmth; collect rain run-off and store it in tanks, dams and swales; and, on a larger scale, keep employment and money circulating in one's bioregion.

Permaculture methods of harnessing natural energies parallel the development of atmospheric ch'i (energy) in Chinese feng shui geomantic traditions. Where ch'i collects in the landscape there will be enhanced fertility and prosperity, predicts feng shui.

Patterns of natural energy flow are used extensively in permaculture design. Circular, spiralling, curving forms are preferred to linear patterns.

Blessing the new Tower of Power, David Lonergan's permaculture jungle, Kangaroo Valley, NSW.

The 'edge effect' of planting areas is increased and enhanced by having wavy or crenelated borders. Increased edge makes for greater availability of light and nutrients, and allows more access. Ponds with wavy edges provide more eco-tones for water life than standard circular ones.

With earthworks, such as road building and ploughing, natural (curving) contour lines are followed, in order to prevent soil erosion and maximise rain penetration. Fence lines are also best run along the contour of the land (otherwise livestock will cause erosion).

Landscape elements are appreciated for their natural functions. For example rocks are useful in their ability to store heat and keep plants warm in winter. Mounds enjoy superior drainage and make ideal garden beds, especially when made from hot compost in cold weather. Geomancers who have studied ancient artificial mounds (dolmen) in Europe believe that they are capable of storing subtle energies and affecting weather, enhancing rainfall and groundwater.

Wilderness values

Richard Webb of Permaculture Asia Ltd in Hong Kong has been studying the tradition and environmental significance of Chinese feng shui groves. These sacred remnant forests are usually found in locations where they help prevent erosion in the water catchment. They also provide a refuge for wildlife and displaced nature spirits.

Since ancient times the sacred tree grove has stood protected from development by spiritual laws in many other parts of the world, and was the province of the Druids in Europe. Groves enhance climate, slow down the movement of wind and water, and thus increase the comfort and protection of people, livestock and crops.

Wilderness zones, important components in permaculture designed properties, can protect important remnant vegetation and provide undisturbed water catchment areas. They are essential for maintaining biodiversity for all the kingdoms of lifeforms, and biodynamic farmer Barbara Hedley refers to them as 'deva stations'.

Geomancy in permaculture

One can embrace a healthy physical and spiritual relationship with the land by practising permaculture from an Earth-spirited perspective. With sensitive landscape design one may easily incorporate geomantic considerations, by initial dowsing plus historical research, if appropriate, to locate subtle energy characteristics and possibly Aboriginal cultural connections. Ideally one seeks prior approval from the spirits of place for the proposed project, meditating on-site at a special energy spot.

Geopathic (harmful Earth energy) zones can be avoided in habitation areas, or harnessed by placing bee hives, compost heaps or Towers of Power there, where they'll thrive. When building design is considered, both fengshui and building biology principles can be used to create healthy, harmonious and unpolluted homes that have a minimal impact on Mother Earth.

Geomancy and permaculture are life enhancing tools with which we can connect to the Earth and Earthspirit in many practical ways, satisfying the emptiness of spirit so prevalent today. With them we can awaken to the dangers of the dominant death culture and be empowered to take action necessary for planetary survival.

References:

'Introduction to Permaculture', Bill Mollison, Tagari, 1991.
'Newsleaf', journal of the BDFGAA in Australia, issue 45, summer 2000.
'Divining Earth Spirit', Alanna Moore, 1994 (now out of print, but being updated in 2001).

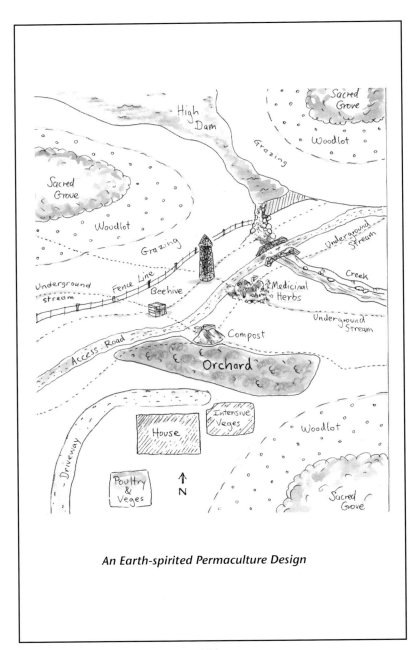

An Earth-spirited Permaculture Design

3:3 *Homodynamics*

by Steven Guth, Canberra.

I've just spent 5 weeks sitting on a pile of dirt floating on a sea of rice paddies. It was located in northern Thailand somewhere between the River Kawi and the Burmese border, with a 40⁰C green house climate. Only about 150km from Bangkok, it was back in the 14th century.

I was in a Monastery sitting at the feet of a Chinese-Thai 'Master', trying to cope with the verbally transmitted esoteric side of Buddhist meditation - how to use guides, how to cloud fly, psychic self-defence, fortune telling, exorcism, self analysis and the viewing of past lives. The system revolves around the accumulation of power. Good breathing is critical, visualisation skills are the key and clairvoyant ability is helpful.

The Monastery was home to about 30 monks and a symbiotic part of the 3000 people village which surrounded it. Thailand is made up of such villages and in total there are 300,000 monasteries in the geographically small 60 million people nation. In the hot, wet fertile rice areas the population density is high. Here villages and monasteries spread like a web over the countryside, as they have done for thousands of years.

In that time the flow of life between people, animals and plants evolved into a system that found its own balance. The spiritual side hides under the guise of Theravada Buddhism and is focused in the Monastery. It took me about 2 weeks to develop the understanding that I present below. I call it Homodynamics because of its similarity to the biodynamic approach. Alas, it is changing rapidly, with chemical fertilizers, pesticides and the rotary hoe altering the natural balances.

At an obvious level, cows have changed from being the honored family member who pulled the plough to merely a family pet. The Monastery had 2, tended by an old monk. In the fields cows were still used to graze on rice stalks, trample weeds and fertilize for the next planting.

Thai cows are very human conscious, far more like Australian dogs than Australian cows. At night they have little smoking fires lit besides them to keep off mosquitoes.

Another example, at a simple level, were the monastery dogs. A motley crew of about 20 animals, they took a week to recognize me and allow me access to my hut. Before that I carried a stick and watched my back. By the third week they kept visitors away from my hut as effectively as they had kept me away. They knew who belonged where. They were fed the huge surplus of food collected by the monks on their morning alms round. They breed at random and nipped within reason.

The Monk's Day

The day started at 4am with the morning bell. I think everyone ignored it until first light at 6am. Then 6 groups of 2 to 4 monks collected together (the word 'assembled' could be used here, but it implies a level of human organization and will that just wasn't there). Each group also had a cart and a boy or 2 from the village to push it.

The boys who came to help the monks had a direct payoff - a huge and varied breakfast. Every street in the village was covered and so all households had a chance to participate in the homodynamic cycle, and 30% did.

The monks were formally dressed in their full robes and walked wth bare feet. The boys ran ahead and yelled "The monks are coming!". Householders came to the road carrying a chalice of boiled rice and a plate of food. The monks stopped and lifted the lid of their begging bowl. Reverently the householder spooned into it a huge dollop of rice.

When I placed rice into a begging bowl it felt like reaching into the stomach, or perhaps the womb, of the Mother Earth - a strange feeling. The rice, I should add, is hand cut from each family's own paddy field, dried under the house and dehulled at the village winnowing mill, half a bag at a time.

The next part of the cycle is heavy breakfast and the feeling of bloat. The monks last meal having finished by 12 noon the day before - a gap of 19 hours between rice loaded meals. Then at 8 am the bell goes off again for the morning's chanting.

The Role of Chanting

Chanting is what village level Buddhism is all about in Thailand. It's done in Pali to a simple rhythm that takes a little for the body to adjust into. Then it helps with meditation. It took me a time to work out that it creates a space for the nature kingdom devas. They come when called by song and, because of centuries of interaction, co-operate to human requests. The Thais, like the Greeks, classify things into water, earth, air and fire.

The chanting hall at my monastery is virtually identical to all the chanting halls in all the other monasteries that spread out through the valley. It is a double cube (like a Masonic temple) built on what I call the Asian yard - about 30 inches. It is 8 units wide, 8 units high and 16 units long, and sits on a cement pedestal 3 units above the growing water level of the surrounding rice paddies. The elaborate roof was roost to hundreds of pigeons that feed off dropped rice.

Evening chanting makes the huge golden Buddha statue radiate with light. The painted scene behind it becomes 'The Deer Park' where 'The Buddha' preached to the novice monks. The scene all comes together and breathes life during the evening chant, during which one can feel the presence of a landscape angel sized water nymph who watches over the surrounding paddy.

To me she appeared whenever asked to, in the form of a water lily flower. She liked to give blessings.

The morning chanting used energy that came from the monks' digestion of their heavy rice-loaded breakfast. As the monks chant and the energy builds up, it rises as a column into the sky. It then spreads out like a cloud to open up and rain down as a million sparkles onto the villagers' rice paddies.

The sparkles float over the paddy water and are drawn back into the chanting hall to be recharged and sent forth again and again. The cycle runs for about 5 minutes. It reminded me of the vortex that is created when biodynamic 500 is stirred in a bucket.

The whole process has been refined over thousands of years. The bare footed monks collecting, the people giving, the monks eating, the monks digesting and the monks chanting. The same chant day after day, for 20, 40 or 50 years of their lives. A symbiotic process - the humans, the paddy, the rice, the animals, the plants and any number of devas and nature spirits all working in an ecological loop for thousands and thousands of years.

The Future?

How long will the yin power of Thai tradition keep it strong, against the destructive extreme yang of the Western ways? Will Thailand remain as one of the few Asian nations to largely escape foreign domination, including the power and influence of China?

Perhaps soon it's systemic harmony will all be gone. The removal of so much Thai forest and the coming of TV, steel, roads, cement and chemicals have altered the balances past the known and well established ancient equilibrium points. A new balance is needed.....

Steven Guth is a geomancer in the Canberra region.
He can be contacted on 02 6288 1070.

3:4 *Agnihotra*

Homa (fire) therapy, originating in ancient Indian Vedic wisdom that was revived in India during the 1940's, is designed to nourish and vitalise nature, as well as neutralise pollution and disease. Homa farms are vibrant with enhanced life energies and have often been transformed from abused and degraded land by this spiritual service to nature. They attract happy birds and bees and provide a healing atmosphere for people too. I visited such a farm, Om Shree Dham, in springtime, 2000.

Serving nature

In the early '90's Lee and Frits Ringma moved away from Sydney to caretake a farm in the Wollombi area of NSW. A small commercial blueberry farm, the owners had been pioneers in introducing the Agnihotra fire ritual to the region and started its regular practice on the farm in 1987. Lee and Frits had been regularly practising Agnihotra themselves since 1989. The farm had prolific growth and a fabulous energy field and they soon developed a great connection with nature from living there. "We wanted to serve nature" Frits said.

Then, in 1994, they were spiritually guided to buy some land nearby. It was a very degraded and neglected property, flogged of goodness from wheat growing. It had also been over-grazed and the compacted sandy ground was concrete hard, with not a worm in sight. No rain could infiltrate and the existing orchard was languishing.

Purification

The atmosphere in the place was so bad that they couldn't stand to go near the filthy house for 3 days. The place was a rubbish dump and they sensed that animals had been tortured there. Lee had initially walked into the house, then went straight out and vomited! It was a huge challenge to cleanse the house and property.

The important initial job was to start doing the sunrise and sunset Agnihotra fires, to remove the bad energy . "The practise of Agnihotra removes the tainted energy layers, peels away the layers of history that lie like dust over the good energy beneath" said Lee.

For 3 days Frits visited and made the special fires at dawn and dusk. After that the energy became clear. The Agnihotra fire, and other supplementary Homas, have been uncovering a latent but powerful energy centre there ever since.

An oasis of life

Now they find it blissful to be on the farm and the good energy there is definitely palpable. Seeds germinate easily and plants establish effortlessly. The place certainly looked lush, cloaked in its spring colours and blossoms, the soil bursting with life. "The whole of nature rejoices when Agnihotra is practised" Frits said.

Local people who, 30 years ago were the owners of the property, came over to marvel at the place a few years back. "How come everything is so green and the soil is so moist?" they asked. Performing the Homas regularly renders the soil more able to hold moisture. A friend who had had much experience of biodynamic farms said she had never seen such healthy, vibrant soil. And even though the region is plagued by rabbits, they are never a problem on this Homa farm.

Agnihotra ash is used all over the farm as a healing tonic. It is sprinkled around the trunks of trees, broadcast over soil and made into a paste, with clay, to fill in wounds or rot in tree trunks. Sick plants enjoy a spray of Agnihotra ash water, which cures disease and increases vitality. Subsequently the plants are abundant with flowers and fruit.

To make this healing spray they fill a copper tub with water and add a handful of ash, then let it sit in the sun for 3 days. This is filtered and put into a spray pack for spraying foliage for up to 3 - 4 times a week until improvement occurs.

Like a blessed oasis, even in a time of drought it can rain just over the farm, which is at the beginning of a valley. "With Agnihotra - nature is more nourished, more balanced and aligned with the source" Frits explained. "With the raising of the vibrations of a place, a feedback of love and gratitude comes from nature. In ancient times they made these fires to maintain abundance in nature and to keep the consciousness of mankind connected to the Divine. Agnihotra draws down Divine energy. It harvests the prana from the solar range and, enlivening the atmosphere, helps the plants and indeed all the kingdoms."

Effects of Agnihotra

The fires are said to neutralise air and other pollution in the atmosphere. Agnihotra ash placed in bodies of water can also be used to counteract pollution, I was told. The improved energetic atmosphere creates an optimum condition for healing people too. Lee and Frits radiated lots of good energy themselves and enjoy travelling around the country, to wherever they are called, to show people the practice of Agnihotra and spread the word. They also help people to clear oppressive, polluted atmospheric conditions with the fires.

"Not only is plant life nourished, but disease is removed from the area and tension is removed from the mind – making all meditation practices easier and the state of unconditional love becomes increasingly available to us. Not only does the performer benefit, but also the household and neighbourhood benefits as stress and pollution are undone" Lee and Frits say. Tests have been done with bacterium cultures in agar-agar. When exposed to the Agnihotra fires the bacteria levels were reduced by 80%. The Homa practice is said to be even effective in clearing radioactive contamination.

The technique

A small fire of dried cow dung is burnt in an inverted copper pyramid of specific dimensions and a Sanskit mantra is uttered, along with a small

offering of rice and ghee into the fire at the precise moment of sunrise and sunset. The mantra that is chanted during the fire ritual is ancient Sanskrit for 'Divine Will be Done'. It all takes about 10 minutes.

The fire is best practised in the centre of a room. The copper pyramid starts collecting healing energies and, if left untouched until the next Agnihotra, except for emptying, will radiate energy continuously.

The pyramid should not sit on plastic or metal (other than copper or gold), which can 'interrupt' the energies, a fact recognised by dowsers such as T.C. Lethbridge. "Metal interferes with the electromagnetic effect of Agnihotra and therefore no metal whatsoever should be kept nearby the copper pyramid" concurs Vasant, in US magazine 'Satsang'.

When performing Agnihotra you are meant to sit square to the pyramid and facing east, with the pyramid kept square to the east, always in the same orientation and sitting level. "It is from the direction of east that the flood of energies, electricites and ethers comes" says Vasant.

During the fire practice healing energies are said to spiral upwards and eastwards out from the pyramid, while they also radiate outwards and are particularly thrust to the north. The best energy is radiated out from the east side, so this is the most healing position to sit at. You can also put a lingam or healing stone or medicinal herbs etc close to the fire to charge them up.

"In addition to other effects" says Vasant" at certain intervals, bursts of energy emanate from the Agnihotra pyramid, depending on the phases of the moon and the position of the Earth in relation to the sun. These bursts of energy thrust nutrients and fragrance through the solar range and have a profound effect on the mind. Tremendous amounts of energy are gathered around the Agnihotra copper pyramid just at Agnihotra time. A magnetic type field is created, one which neutralises negative types of energy and reinforces positive types of energy".

I could relate to these statements myself because, when attending an Agnihotra fire one afternoon, I perceived bursts of energy pulsing out from the pyramid towards me, even before the fire had begun.

At the precise times of sunrise and sunset there are special energies coming into play which are acted upon. These energies provide 'windows of opportunity' says Lee. Scientific investigation at stone circles in England- the Dragon Project- also reveals interesting energy patterns at these times, with anomalies in the ultrasonic and infrared sphere for a start. Other special or complimentary Homas are conducted at the full and new moon times, some running for 24 hour long stretches.

During these Homas prana is said to be drawn down from the solar range into the environment and the existent prana, depleted and distorted by pollution, is brought back into balance, into an ideal state. "Vitality and subtle nourishment is drawn into the environment on an enormous scale, enabling nature to heal itself. The basic effect reaches up to 12 km (8 miles) into the atmosphere and up to one kilometre (.7 mile) around the copper pyramid" Lee said.

Homa farms elsewhere

Homa centres and farms are found around the world. I was told of great successes with farms in Peru. 'Panama evil', a fungal infection, was wiping out plantain (banana) crops and the farmers were told that nothing more could be done, because the fungus was rife in the atmosphere. Many farmers were abandoning their diseased crops and sick land, having tried every chemical that government agencies recommended, without success. But with the application of Homa therapy they have enjoyed total rejuvenation of the farms. American Homa therapists approached the farmers and, under the observation of government and scientific bodies, trained the farmers in Homa techniques free of charge.

To reinforce the basic Agnihotra fires in such highly diseased areas, extra Homas and techniques are recommended. A related Homa practice, with different mantras is performed daily to fortify the energy field created by Agnihotra.

On a farm or in a garden Agnihotra is usually practised at the centre point and you can also place a pyramid in each of the 4 directions along boundaries. When Agnihotra is performed, these pyramids will resonate with the central fire and amplify its effects many fold.

A resonant point can also be established on the farm by placing an inverted copper pyramid, charged with certain mantras, that is buried a half metre (18") underground, with another, charged with different mantras, placed directly above it on a column of soil. This helps to anchor the energies even more.

On the Peruvian farms, the Homa resonance point was installed and the farmers began to practise the basic fires twice daily. "After only a week I began to observe that my plantain trees began to develop very green healthy leaves" one farmer reported. After 4 months of the Homa therapy the pathogens had all disappeared and there was a subsequent increase in production, with bigger crops of larger fruit with better taste, colour and texture. The vegetative cycle was also shortened by 40%.

Neighbouring plantations also registered rejuvenating effects and people with conditions such as asthma and skin problems were finding, after sitting by the fires and inhaling the healing smoke, and also applying ash to themselves mixed with ghee, that they were experiencing all sorts of remarkable healing. A pinch of ash taken internally every day can be great prophylactic medicine.

'Pillars of fire'

Stone lingams are a feature of the gardens at Om Shree Dham. 'Shiva lingams' are egg shaped stones found in certain holy rivers of India. They have long been revered as generators of divine energy and are kept in temples and ashrams throughout India. The lingam is usually kept standing upright in a special hollowed out stone base, which represents the 'yoni' or feminine aspect of divinity (and the goddess Shakti).

The lingams represent the unmanifest from which creation is born. Usually of a yang nature, they are sometimes referred to as 'pillars of

fire'. The Narmada lingams are said to have a perfect yin/yang energy balance. Meditation with such a lingam is facilitated, because it is ' a tuning device into the higher self'. It can help to awaken one's kundalini force and give freedom from subconscious patterning, I was told.

Sizes range from little pendant sized lingams, which, if worn constantly, have a permanent healing influence on the aura; to great omphalos types at 1 m (1 yd) or so tall, which can act as energy generators for entire regions. These earthy coloured stones often have beautiful patterns and are said to be formed of a combination of basalt, agate and quartz. There are several large ones installed in the ACT, Victoria and Queensland and some have been positioned to act as 'interplanetary energy portals'.

Lee and Frits' beautiful lingams from India's holy Narmada River. This river is likened to a Universal Mother Goddess, who is the nurturing, nourishing aspect of Divinity.

"Interestingly" they have written "when clairvoyants are tuning into this holy river through her lingam stones, they see red water. What they are actually perceiving is the colour of vital prana or life-force, in other words – spiritual fire."

When meditating, the idea is to cup the lingam in your lap, with the right hand under the left, allowing the lingam to rest upright against the abdomen. This helps to free the flow of energies up the spine and focus on the ever deepening awakening of the heart chakra. "Like cosmic receiving stations, under the principle of 'like attracts like' the giant lingams channel healing to Mother Earth, helping to raise the kundalini of the planet" I was told.

Parallels

I could see many parallels here to the use of Towers of Power (symbolic of fire energy and working with the yang forces), which harness the sun's energy and help to make it rain. "Being charged by fire means manifesting the energy of clarity" says Roseline Deleu, in relation to feng shui principles. Irish Round Towers have been associated with ancient fire temples belonging to the goddess Bride/Bridget.

Towers of Power can help to neutralise electro-magnetic radiation from nearby power lines, according to my dowsing. So it was not surprising to learn that electro-magnetic radiation can be neutralised by Agnihotra, as well as radioactivity and bacterial activity.

The practise of biodynamics seems related too. The Agnihotra ash acts like a biodynamic fertiliser and is good to add to soil and compost heaps. "Yes, biodynamics works very well with Agnihotra. In fact – if you put a pinch of the ash from the Agnihotra fire into the liquid 500, this will decrease the stirring time by half" Frits said.

You can find out more about Homa farms and Homa therapy, as well as Narmada lingams and more from Lee and Frits Ringma at 'Om Shree Dham', PO Box 68 Cessnock 2325, ph/fax 02 4998 1332, mobile 0418 643 489, email: omshreedham@hunterlink.com.au

There is also a 'Satsang Australia' magazine which they are a contact for.

Find out about the Homa Therapy Association of Australia: http://www.summit.net/home/ Agnihotra

A garden lingam at Om Shree Dham.

PART FOUR: TOWER TECHNOLOGY

4:1 Ireland's Magical Heritage

Fairy Stories?

Before my research trip to Ireland in April 2000 I did some homework on where I could see interesting, ancient sites, as well as the Round Towers, which were my primary interest. I was amazed to learn of the vast numbers of ancient sites recorded. For instance, the ringfort (circular earth-walled) settlements number around 50,000. There are more ancient sites in Ireland, I learned, than anywhere in Europe, and 60% of Europe's rock art is found on this island.

"It's because the Irish are so superstitious", my ex-patriate-Irish dowser friend Sandy Griffin explained. He illustrated his point with this story.

As a young man working in rural Ireland in the 1940's, he was once walking down a country lane with another young man who was a firewood supplier. They were passing by an old ring fort, covered by an ancient, gnarled old hawthorn grove. The trees were mostly dead, with very thick trunks.

"Would you know of any good firewood around here?" Sandy asked. "Ah, no. Nothing around here" was the reply. "But what about all that?" he asked, pointing to the ring fort. "Oh, that ! You can't cut those down, they're the homes of the fairies. They dance around them at night!" he said, intoning that 'wasn't that obvious?' Sandy thought it quite amusing at the time, that a grown lad still believed in fairies.

 When I arrived in Dublin and discussed this with Sandy's cousin's family they were much more to the point. "It is the fairies which protect the sites!" Not just the belief in them, I noted. Fairies, it turns out, in the Irish view of things, are not always the happy little sprites we have been led to believe.

They can also be fierce guardians of their homes. Demolish a Bronze Age barrow mound or ancient tree grove and beware the consequences!

Ireland's ancient belief system, which has survived to this day in many ways, is greatly exemplified in those stories which we have inherited as 'fairy tales'. They give fascinating insights into a land where the veils between the spirit world and the physical are often quite thin, particularly on certain days and in certain places. There is a strong fear that the fairies will be offended by some environmentally unsound action and steal away your spirit, for enslavement in the fairy kingdoms, or other such punishment.

One story describes how someone built an extension to his house on the wrong side, where it interfered with a fairy pathway. Despite being warned by a man who was a friend of the fairies, he went ahead, and consequently suffered dire results.

These stories serve to reinforce the need to leave undisturbed the important geomantic points and pathways in the landscape. And, much like Australian Aboriginal stories have long kept inquisitive people away from dangerous, sacred or taboo places, they have proved very successful.

In the 1850's one third of Australia's population originated from the Emerald Isle, so it is interesting to learn that some part of the white Australian mindset shares beliefs common with Aboriginal tradition. Unfortunately the Irish in Australia at the time were largely victims of cultural genocide by the English, so their rich history and cultural traditions have been mostly ignored in the dominant paradigm of our Anglo-centric heritage.

The long history of Ireland

Where did Ireland's magical traditions originate? Some say it was in a legendary lost continent of Atlantis, that once existed in the Atlantic Ocean.

The history books tell of many waves of colonisation in Ireland's early days and these have been recorded in the ancient Annals. The earliest recorded Irish stories were written some 200-500 years after the formal end of paganism, so they don't properly represent oral traditions, but merely echo the spirit of the pagan era.

From the Book of Migrations and the Book of Invasions, we learn of the long series of migrations of different groups, going back before the time of the Flood. Tribes with advanced technology initially came from the western sea (Atlantis, perhaps) and carried on through Europe, the Caucasus mountains, then India, finally to return to Ireland thousands of years later, according to Atlantean researcher Helen O'Cleary.[1] The earliest Celtic language and the Indian Sanskrit language have many words and phrases in common, while Irish Gaelic is one of the oldest languages in Europe.

The first invasion on record was that of the Nemedians, before the Flood (which may refer to the catastrophe which engulfed Atlantis, possibly some 10,000 or so years ago; or was it just the rising sea levels of the ending of last ice age?). Known as the Sons of the Sun, they were tall (later becoming known as giants) with piercing eyes and magic powers that could calm storms. Their silver ships were decorated with painted eyes and serpents, their sacred symbols.

The next invasion was the Fomorian tribe, more mighty sea giants, who came just after the Flood. They were said to be descended from Noah, and were led by Lady Banbha with her 50 maidens and 3 men. The Fomorians were also credited with great magical powers over nature. They were renowned as megalith builders, credited with the construction of cyclopean walls, standing stones and stone circles, whilst being preoccupied with solar symbols.[16] The great Round Tower at Kilmacduagh, seen on the cover of this book, has cyclopean style masonry work.

Perhaps the magical technology of the Fomorians originally derived from an advanced civilisation in the Sirius star system, as the 50 maidens story could be referring to the 50 year Sirius cycle. According to author Robert Temple, groups of 50 gods / goddesses bringing cultural advancement is a common theme in Sirius related myth from diverse regions. [3]

Later on, Partholan people from Spain clashed with the Fomorians, who fought them fiercely on the central Irish plains and were defeated. After 400 years more warrior tribes overran the Emerald Isle. The Fir-bolgs came and defeated the Partholan, and it was they who divided Ireland into four quarters plus one central province.

Soon after came the Tuatha de Danaan - the children of the goddess

Dana. This tribe may be linked with the Danaoi people of Greece, who also called themselves the children of the goddess Dana. [4]

Dana/Danu was once a goddess of great universality. She is a goddess of the earliest Indian pantheon, later being considered the enemy of Indra, the king of the Gods, in the Rig Veda. In the Celtic language Don/ Danu is linked to floodwater and in Sanskrit it is the word for streams of water. In Celtic mythology Don was the esteemed goddess of wisdom, astronomy, water, agronomy and hills and high places. Other sources say that Danu was originally a river goddess, whose name is found in many great rivers of Europe – the Danube, Don and Dnieper.

The Tuatha de Danaan were tall and fair haired, and credited with great knowledge of maritime and metallurgy skills, and great supernatural powers. A tradition cites their origins from a sunken island called Murias. The tribe brought with them their 3 most precious relics or symbols.

These were the sacred chalice of rejuvenation and rebirth, later mythologised as the cauldron of inspiration of Celtic goddesses, and later still as the Holy Grail of Christianity; the spear of the mighty sun god Lugh (who could destroy whole armies with fire); and the Lia Fail, a sacred stone that radiated boundless magical energies, and was associated with cosmic forces. [2]

Lia Fail/Stone of Destiny, Hill of Tara.

These ancients races must have known of the energetic forces inherent in rocks. Across Ireland and Britain the traditional link between ceremonial stones and sovereignty remains strong. The granite Lia Fail at Ireland's holy hill of Tara could convey kingship, and any new king had to be first approved by the local Earth Mother goddess Maeve, who communicated her approval through the stone. However the stone at Tara is not in it's original position and has no special energy patterns apparent to my dowsing. It may not even be the original Lia Fail. There is another Stone of Destiny associated with Westminster Abbey and the Scottish throne.

But stones can definitely hold strong memory patterns, which are not only apparent to a dowser, as is evident from an interesting anecdote. A stone once turned up in a post parcel at a tour company in England, with a note from a Belgian archeologist. The man said that he had taken the stone from Clava Cairn and felt that he'd been cursed ever since this had occurred. He was now wanting it returned it to it's rightful location. [5]

Religious evolution

The pagan farmers of neolithic Ireland honoured their landscape as being the home of a multitude of spirit beings, integral to the life force of place. They had ritual practices which sought to appease the local fairies, gods and goddesses, to ensure good harvest and health to all. If they did not maintain proper respect and homage to the spirit of place, they believed, all sorts of mischief might be unleashed.

The Irish recognised special power centres, of intense Earth spirit, which became their places of Earth spirit communion. They worshipped it's local manifestations at wells, springs, caves and special stones. Every region had it's own autonomous gods and goddesses, for there was no formal or centralised religion.

We can guess that the general purpose of their spiritual activity was focussed on the ceremonial cyclic renewal and harmonisation of the energy of place. It was about ritually fusing the energies of sky and earth, in the alchemical

 marriage of yin and yang. Thus they invited the energies of the sun, moon and planets to combine with the strong Earth spirit, in order to boost regional fertility and balance. The 4 cardinal points and probably the 4 elements were honoured as sacred too, and may be what is depicted on the ringed cross.

The incoming Celtic peoples (circa 650-300BC) also believed that spirits inhabited the landscape and dictated the health and fertility of the land. Local deities were often renamed by the Celts and these were then referred to by other (foreign) names in the records of visiting academics. Many of the earliest deities were originally female and became male later on, when patriarchal values were on the rise. So there's a confusing tapestry of deity names.

119

The traditional tribal shamen (clever men) of earlier times, evolved into the Druid classes, and this intelligentsia were responsible for education, magic, ritual and literary developments. They were renowned abroad for their wisdom. Later the Christian monks would have probably taken over some of the Druids' roles.

Diodorus Suculus, the Greek scholar, had reported circa 44BC that Apollo was the chief god in Ireland who visited the island once in 19 years. "The worship of Apollo" he wrote, "is preferred to that of any other god and, as they daily celebrate this deity with songs of praise and worship him with the highest honours, they are considered as peculiarly the priests of Apollo, whose sacred grove and singular temple of round form, endowed with many gifts, are there."

O' Brien cites this as proof of the early existence of Round Towers and we don't know if Round Tower prototypes, built of wood, could have been around in those times. More likely the 'singular temples of round form' referred to stone circles.

Apollo is associated with the sun and is said to have invented and played the harp, which the early Irish all played skilfully. The Welsh learned it from them. Orpheus, another divine harpist of the ancients, played music which was said to 'stay the course of rivers, lull the listening woods, move the stones into prescribed positions and tame the savageness of man'. Orpheus was originally of eastern origin. Was there once a secret knowledge of the power of sound and how it could be harnessed for the elevation of the massive megaliths into their positions in the stone circles? [2]

The substitution of deities in myths to fit the political correctness of the times was also evident in the Christian era. Robert Graves suggests that Jesus was simply Apollo revisited. During the reign of Constantine (an ex-Sol Invinctus follower) the solar symbols of Apollo and Mithras were transferred to Christ and from then on church altars were oriented to the east (as they had been in pagan temples for other reasons). The Buddha in the east was also symbolised by the sun.

As for the Sirius connection, elements common to the Sirius myth keep on popping up. Apollo was sometimes a sea dweller, associated with the sacred dolphin (wisdom fish). Jesus's Mary had watery connotations (all very Piscean age) while John the Baptist is apparently based on the ancient Sumerian fish god Oannes, as was a later god Poseidon; while Peter was associated with fishermen. Poseidon was the ruler of Atlantis, according to Plato. [7]

The Sumerians half-man half-fish god Oannes led 50 culture bringers - the Anunnaki, and this myth is connected to the the later Jason and the (50) Argonauts myth. Sirius B revolves around Sirius A every 50 years, a fact known to the Dogon. According to Robert Temple, stories like these, and other which involve groups of 50 people, apparently preserve the concept that some of our ancestors, or culture, came from the Sirius star system. [3]

According to Euripides, the Pelasgian people, says Robert Lewis, adopted the title of Danaans and claimed birth from 'the serpent's teeth', which is a kind of code for the Sirius star system. The Egyptian hieroglyphic for Sirius, whose rising heralded the annual floods and new year and towards

 which the pyramids were oriented, also happens to be a 'serpent's tooth'. [5] According to O' Brien, the 'tooth of the dragon' is an allegory of human origins, of the spontaneous appearance of an advanced race.

The west African Dogon tribe equivalent of Oannes is Nommo, the 'monitor of the universe', an amphibious culture hero who set up society on Earth as the 'Instructor of the New World'. Nommo's place, the Sirius star system, was known by the Dogon as the land of fish. Nommo's planet is known as 'pure earth' whereas our Earth is regarded as impure, and we the impure Fox race, the outcast. To atone for our impurity the Nommo dies and is resurrected on a tree as a sacrifice, in order to purify and cleanse Earth. He even had a Eucharistic meal for humanity, before resurrection. Nommo will come again when a certain star appears, say the Dogon.

The Dogon have amazing astronomical knowledge, their history and legends going back over 5000 years and related to pre-dynastic Egypt (from whence they emigrated at that time). Their profound knowledge of the distant Sirius system was only recently confirmed by modern western astronomers. They also knew that Saturn has a ring around it, that our planets go around the sun, that Jupiter has 4 moons, etc, etc. All this was brought to the attention of the west by 2 French anthropologists who spent 4 years with them researching their beliefs. They were eventually given the Dogons' most secret knowledge, after a special meeting of elders decided to pass it on to them. [3]

There is an Aboriginal tribe in South Australia who also trace their origins to the Sirius star system and this is said to be recorded in a sacred cave.

The Mesopotamian culture had advanced knowledge of the stars and astrological systems. It is clear, also, from archeological finds that detailed astronomical knowledge was incorporated into ancient monuments of England and Ireland.

An inkling of the intellectual heritage possessed by the Irish is evident when we read that the Irish saint Virgile in the 8th century was tried for heresy because he claimed that the Earth was round and that a continent lay to the west. He produced maps of the Atlantic Ocean which are said to be kept at the Vatican.[7]

Sun worship

Particular fascination with the sun by the megalithic peoples of Europe's western seaboard is evident when we realise that many of the stone circles, built over a period of about 2000 years, were carefully aligned to show the midsummer and midwinter sunrise and sunset. Many of them were hundreds of years in the making and are precision instruments that are unique expressions of people and place.

Sun worship must have really taken off when, around 1400BC, the Irish/ English climate grew colder and wetter. Before this time it was more like the south of France there. Many agricultural districts became ruined and ecosystems collapsed around this time. The moors of Devon and Cornwall and the Scottish highlands, once all covered in healthy forests, were destroyed by pre-historic farming practices, coupled with this climatic change. [6]

Goddesses of the sun

The sun was revered as the ultimate force of fertility and the earliest sun deities were mostly female, while the moon was traditionally masculine. However "all too often the female sun deities are not acknowledged". [8]

The sun was regarded as feminine until the 16ᵗʰ century in England.

Brigid is the great triple goddess of the Celtic Irish, who in Britain was known as Brigantia, Bride in Scotland, Brigandu in Brittany and possibly Britomartis in Crete. One of goddess Brigid's aspects ruled smithcraft/metal forging, one ruled poetry and inspiration, for which purpose she carried a famous cauldron, and her third identity was as goddess of healing and medicine. Her unified symbol was fire and she was known as 'bright arrow' or 'the bright one'. Some think of her as an aspect of the goddess Danu.

As well as light and fire, Brigid was also identified with the Earth and the soil's fertility. 'St Brigid' was probably fabricated from 2 earlier native goddesses, for she is the only saint to have 2 holy days dedicated to her. Saint Brigid's attributes match those of the earlier goddess/ goddesses.

Woven Bridget's crosses, Dublin Museum.

St Brigid's day of February 1ˢᵗ (Imbolc) was traditionally the time of preparation for the season's planting, and when the corn dolly, made at the Lughnasadh harvest festival, was ritually ploughed in. No work was allowed to be done that involved the turning of wheels. People made St Brigid crosses from rushes, straw, wood or feathers and these were hung from doors to protect a family from illness and misfortune. Brigid also presided over May Day celebrations. [9] Her brass shoe was the most sacred object imaginable and men were barred from her sanctuary.

Aine (pronounced Onya) is a great goddess of ancient Ireland, surviving as the queen of the fairies of south Munster. She was originally a sun-goddess, whom, in the form of Lair Derg, the red mare, none could outrun. There was a special feast for her at midsummer's night, when farmers carried torches of straw in procession around Knockainy and waved them over the cattle and fields for protection and fruitfulness; and she has a sacred lake. Eventually Aine disappeared into Knockainy Hill, where she is said to still live in a splendid castle.

Elsewhere in the ancient world there were female sun dieties, such as Sol, the Icelandic goddess of the sun. Sunnu was the Scandinavian's 'mistress sun'. This 'bright bride of heaven' had a special function of 'elf beam' or 'deceiver of dwarfs', for these beings are petrified by her glance. Stone was important to her in another way - her worshippers carved stone circles across the landscape as part of her sacred rites.

Saule was the Baltic people's greatest goddess (Lithuanian and Latvian) - the shining sun, sky weaver, amber goddess. Meness was the male moon deity there. Sekhmet is Egypt's lion headed sun goddess, she was very aggressive and went on murder rampages, as you might expect a sun goddess from a harsh, hot climate to do. [8]

The Sun and the Cross

Circles and wheels have been globally used as symbols to denote the sun deity since ancient times. The ringed cross in Ireland was once regarded as a sign of harmony, its vertical and horizontal elements representing the cosmic opposites of heaven and earth, light and dark, life and death. And perhaps the 4 quarters and 4 elements also. It also represented the sun goddess herself, until she was reinvented as St Bridget, when it became known as St Bridgit's cross. A ringed cross is found above the lintelled doorway of the Round Tower at Antrim, which Lalor considers to be one of the earliest Towers. The ringed cross has also been associated with the tree of life and European nature worship. [10]

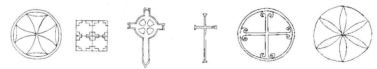

The so-called Celtic cross pre-dates Christianity by some 1500 years. So the cross is a symbol of great antiquity and is apparent in many forms, from small to monumental. A remarkable menhir (megalith) of great antiquity found in County Donegal was said to have 4 cups carved into it "so arranged that the channels extending from them form a perfect cross of the Roman character". [11]

The magnificent standing stones of Callanish, off the coast of Scotland, were originally marking out a huge cross pattern, with a central chambered cairn that has been dated to 2000BC. Local beliefs maintain that on the dawn of midsummer's day the 'Shining One' walks down Callanish's 270 foot long stone avenue. [12] I suppose the shining one would have originally been the local solar deity, whoever she or he was.

The intricately carved stone High Crosses at the monasteries were thought to have been erected inside the church at the cardinal points and at the entrances to monastic enclosures, to act as barriers against evil and as focal points for the people gathered outside at church services. [6]

High cross and Round Tower.

Fire

Fire has been used universally as a symbol for the sun, and fire festivals were once common in Ireland. Lughnasadh (Lammas) is the most popular of ancient festivities in Ireland. Held on August 1st it celebrates the time when Lugh, the god of light weds Eire, the fair Earth. People celebrated the harvest of the crops with fires lit on hilltops as well as races, contests, feasting and lovemaking.

The Roman goddess of fire was Vesta and on March 1st the vestal virgins re-lit her perpetual fire by rubbing sticks together. A goddess of generation, she was honoured as a mother, and had phallic effigies adorning her temples until the days of imperial Rome.

Some scholars have considered that Irish Round Towers could have been sacred fire towers, although there is no physical evidence of fire being used inside them.

Lunar orientation

The moon was originally seen as a masculine deity, hence the 'man in the moon' of English tradition. Moon planting follows the observation that plant growth can be stimulated by planting just before full moon and at certain lunar positions. Water in the environment is also under the influenced of the moon and lunar reckoning was once an obviously important activity. Stone circles generally reflect this. Some, like Stonehenge, depict the extreme positions of moonrise and moonset in the 18.61 year lunar cycle (known to the Greeks as the Metonic cycle or Great Year), which has only relatively recently been realised by modern observers.

Lunulae, Dublin Museum

The Irish fashioned 'lunulae' – fabulous neck collars made of finely wrought silver and gold, some 3 - 4000 years ago. These are considered to have lunar calculations etched into their ornamentation, and must have been highly prized accessories of the Druid intellectuals.

Perhaps Apollo, who Diodorus said returned to Ireland every 19 years, could have been confused with a moon god? Or perhaps the sun and moon were always paired together? St Brigid's fire temple at Kildare had 19 priestess/nun tending the fire.

Irish Olympics

Taillte was the goddess of August, the foster mother of the light, embodied in the god Lug. One of the greatest of Earth goddesses, she lived on the magical hill of Tara, where she had directed the clearing of an immense forest, the wood of Cuan, creating in a month the Plain of Oenach. Taillten, where she built her palace, is today's Telltown, near Kells, County Meath.

An annual festival in her honour once lasted all of August, complete with mercantile fairs and sporting events, right up till mediaeval times. The festival eventually died out, but early in the 20th century, in an attempt to revive Irish culture, the Tailltean Games were restored for a while.

A Round Tower at Teamor, near Telltown, was once at the focus of this so-called 'Irish Olympics'. O'Brien said that this was at a place where Druids had originally sacrificed, in honour of the sun and moon, heaven and earth, on August 1st - Lugh-Nasa, meaning the anniversary of the sun, being the fifth moon after the vernal equinox. At this time young people were given in marriage, as the festival celebrated the marriage of the sun and moon. So, not surprisingly, this festival was also called the Matrimonial Assembly, while poets called it the Festival of Love.

Egypt also has a Tailtal (Tail is Irish for wife) which is known for the same things and in other parts of the world one finds identical games held over the same 30 days. The name of the Eleusinian Mysteries was also Tailtine, noted O'Brien. [2]

Fire and Water

The combined sanctity of fire and water is a very ancient Indo-European tradition. The 2 elements are linked by the sacred cauldron, which is a symbol common to many European cultures. Welsh goddess Ceridwen's Cauldron would brew the spark of inspiration, while the Holy Grail became a Christianised version, with a lot or romantic adventures added on.

England had a goddess who presided over both fire and water. Sulis, an ancient healing goddess, has a special shrine at Bath. Some think her a solar deity, deriving her name from a word meaning 'sun' and 'eye', and this may account for perpetual fires kept at her shrines, and may be the reason why only hot springs were hers. Sulis was thought to descend into the springs underground at night. A rare Celtic coin found at Bath shows this sun goddess.

Her name is from the same root word for sun that is seen in sun goddess names Saule, Solntse, Suil. Sulis has a triple form, the Suliviae, as one inscription at Bath attests, and this is also seen at water shrines in France. Romans called her Minerva Medica. When the Romans took over the spring at Bath from the Celts they replaced the sun goddess with the god Apollo and carved his image in the stone temple pediment.

The Basques have a woman sun and there is the belief that evil is exorcised by her fiery power. On midsummer's eve people went to a high place to keep a night vigil, then hailed the sunrise with songs and greetings. Then the people would rush to the nearest spring to bathe in the specially infused waters, for they believed that the sun's fire infused the waters with fecundity and healing, especially of skin problems. They would also bathe in the morning dew, and these customs were also observed in the Baltic countries. Solstice night bonfires were also lit and used to rekindle the hearth fires of the villagers.

Many Irish holy wells are associated with sun goddess Grian in living tradition. Tobar na Greine (pronounced Gronya) is the Well of the Sun, with waters said to be curative of eye ailments. 'Sunstones' were ritual offerings made to gain favours that were placed on an altar or dropped into the spring. Sunstones were pebbles of white quartz, for in Ireland this is the stone of the sun. Crystal was used by Scottish clans to sanctify water and the Hindus also traditionally assign crystal to the sun.

Christianised traditions include well 'patterns' which involve ritual circumnavigation sunwise around a holy well, often on all fours or knees.

The eye is a symbol often found carved at ancient stone monuments, and associated with sun worship. It could also be depicting the vesica pisces/ mandorla common to ancient British, as well as Greek and Egyptian culture. This symbol may reflect a part of the knowledge of sacred geometry.

Red and white rags were often made as offerings at holy wells, left in trees and thus removing one's ailments as they rotted. Red and white, seen on the maypole and common at sun/fire festivals, are colours pertaining to the sun.[12] An Irish friend says that in her childhood the colours red and white were associated with death and sorcery. A good Catholic girl would not want to be associated with the sun goddess, after all!

Until only recently in Yorkshire and Lincolnshire there lingered a tradition known as 'wading the water'. A bucket was left out on the eve of Easter day to reflect the rays of the rising sun. If the waters 'waded', that is rippled, then this was taken as an omen of rain.

Cup shaped hollows carved into megaliths and bullaun stones (see page 149) at ancient Irish sacred sites might have once held water for this same purpose – to ceremonially welcome the beginning of the agricultural cycle and spring planting time, and invite the solar energies to spark fire into the water of the Earth, via the medium of air - ritually combining the 4 sacred elements of life. Water collecting in the hollows is usually traditionally deemed curative.

A 9 holed bullaun stone at County Cavan, is found in the immediate vicinity of a very sacred well called 'Tober Brigid'. "It seems to me that our bullauns, as a rule, are found curiously associated with certain springs or wells usually esteemed holy" wrote W. F. Wakeman in 1891. This 'St Brigid's Stone', Wakeman recorded, was associated with the tradition of cursing stones. The greatest concentration of bullauns is at Glendalough, and the greatest number there are found near the pilgrimage road, being on both sides of the river leading from the Wicklow Gap to the monastery. [11]

As water is known to be capable of retaining memory, and even responds to our thoughts and feelings [13], perhaps the bullauns were once used like primitive radionic devices, and were designed to capture and store particular energies, at certain special moments in time, in the sacred spring water.

Beltaine

Springtime celebrated with the Maypole in Australia.

The worship of Bel, the Irish sun god/goddess was still prevalent when St Patrick arrived in Ireland. The Irish name for May Day is Bealtaine, or Bel's fire. On May day eve bonfires were lit in Bel's honour all over Scotland, Wales and Ireland and cattle driven through them to ward off disease.

May Day originally celebrated the origin of creation, with festivities also found in Persia, India and Egypt. The permanent village Maypole tradition with ribbon dancing was a 19th century revival and originally festivities were much more raunchy and known for 'greenwood marriages'. It had once been the tradition for young people to pair up and spend the night together on the eve of May 1st.

At dawn a tree was cut down and set up in the village, or else the house was decorated with fresh branches. The May king or queen would go on procession, taking fresh branches to the households, to celebrate the revivified spirit of spring, and they would be thanked and rewarded.

Thus the Maypole is linked to the Tree of Life, a symbol common to many cultures.

Festivities at Beltaine also typically included a sun vigil on a high place, where the sun was encouraged to come out of the darkness with the help of bonfires until sunrise.

129

There was a tradition that the sun danced at the Mayday sunrise (also at midsummer and Easter) but it should never be looked at directly. So people viewed the sun via its reflection in a water mirror. People set bowls of water on the threshold to catch the rising sun's rays.

By shaking the dishes, the rippling water thus allowed the sunlight to dance on the walls and ceilings, and so the powerful rays of the goddess would be invoked to protect and purify the house.

Sacred Dance

The May pole originates from a time in many folk traditions when "the tree of life was the world axis, linking heaven and Earth and providing the pathway for shamanic ascent to the heavens" notes Maria-Gabriele Wosien.

Worshippers did circular dances around their sacred buildings and monuments, mimicking the motion of the planets, as "the sacred dance is an expression of identification with the eternal cyclic patterns of the cosmos, the creative forces of heaven in eternal motion revolving around a still centre. It is an essential part of religious tradition the world over and was vital to early Christian worship," says Wosien.[14] However dance traditions were eventually outlawed in Christian practice, while some survived in pockets.

'Clipping the church' was a tradition once enacted each St Brigid's Day, which echoed the custom of the original feast day of Imbolc, when ritual dance at sacred standing stones was the custom.[15] Church 'clipping', meaning to clasp or embrace, involved people holding hands and singing as they walked around the church in a clockwise direction - the 'way of the sun', or forming a circle and advancing and retreating three times.

The tradition was maintained in Birmingham until 1800 and in many other churches it didn't die out until the 19th century. In Radnorshire, Wales, churchyards were places of dancing, games, feasts and revels, and this was common in other parts of Wales; while in Shropshire games in the churchyard of Stoke St Milborough were still held in 1820. In Painswick Gloucestershire clipping has been revived in modern times, followed by an open-air clipping sermon, delivered from the base of the church tower.

The Romans had a festival – Lupercalia, which included sacred dance around the altar.

In some churches from the 11th century annual dances were held on labyrinth designs laid out on the church floor of the nave or near the western door. [14]

Sacred walks

The 'Beating of the Bounds' was an annual ritual, where people would walk the parish or property boundaries, often stopping at pre-Christian monuments along the way and once giving offerings or making sacrifices at specific points to appease the local spirits of place.

'The Way of the Cross' is a processional walk that symbolically marks out the stations of the cross. The congregation often winds up a hill, marking the stations in ascending sequence, in other places they make a circuit around the church, ending up at the altar.

Holy wells

There are some 3000 holy wells in Ireland and many pilgrimage patterns on the patron (saint) days were held at these wells, usually in the last fortnight in July or the first fortnight in August. Such festivities were originally dedicated to the god of the harvest in pagan times. Many of the wells were dedicated to St Brigid.

The Church eventually suppressed many of these 'patterns' at holy wells because of the debauchery and faction fights that went on in the evenings, after the pious practises had finished. Patterns were often associated with the sacred sites of older times – with pilgrims visiting bullauns, sacred trees, stone cairns and pillar stones.

In searching for motives behind such pilgrimage to the holy wells, 18th century antiquarian Rev. Charles O'Conor asked an old man who used to visit wells in Roscommon. He explained that – "his ancestors always did it; that it was a preservative against the sorceries of the Druids; that their cattle were preserved by it from infections and disorders; that the fairies were kept in good humour by it" and that penance was done by it, as well as personal cures, with individual wells pertaining to different ailments, even madness.

At one holy well at Kilbarry, Roscommon, patients slept on stone slabs, called 'saint's beds' in a regime similar to treatment provided for the ancient Greeks by the healing god Ascepius at Epidauros and elsewhere. [16]

The Druids

The intellectual caste in Ireland were known as Druids. Later, in Christian times they were referred to as Culdees, which is said to mean magic workers. Confusingly, this group spawned a Christian reformist movement around the time of the Round Tower building phase, and thus it was the Culdees who some say are responsible for them.

Knowing the high standard of Druid learning, St Patrick found that both cults taught similar concepts. They both believed in survival after death and an in-dwelling spirit. The Druids even had a deity, a chief of the tree spirits, called Hesus/Esus who was sacrificed on the oak tree.

According to Robert Lewis, before the "Essenes' invention of Jesus" the Druids at Glastonbury (site of the first Christian church in England) were "annually crucifying a god - Hesus (Hu) on tors and hilltops. Hesus was a law bringer, one of a trinity with Beli/Belenus (the sun) and Taran/Taranus". [5]

Despite the common ground, St Patrick encountered hostile resistance to his religious imperialism. To make his points heard he was responsible for the destruction of many standing stones (that he incorrectly called 'idols') and any objects dedicated to the sun.

He also wiped out many volumes of books of Druid knowledge, so it is difficult to know precisely just what the Druids got up to. The Druid colleges were taken over and these became the monasteries and nunneries.

Ireland's magical past seemed doomed to be over, but with the advent of the Round Towers it seems to be somewhat irrepressible, even if probably unintentional!

References:

1- 'Atlantis in Ireland, Round Towers of Ireland'. Henry O'Brien. Steiner Books, USA, originally published in 1834.

2- 'The Sirius Mystery'. Robert Temple. Sidgwick and Jackson, London, 1976.

3- 'The Book of Druidry'. Ross Nichols. Thorsons, London, 1990.

4 - 'Northern Earth' – Journal of the Northern Earth Mysteries group, UK, No 81.

5- 'The 13th Stone', Robert Lewis, Fountainhead Press, 1997.

6- 'The Irish Round Tower, origins and architecture explored', Brian Lalor, The Collins Press, 1999.

7- 'Atlantis,' Helen O'Cleary, Pegasus, London, 1971.

8- 'Eclipse of the Sun', Janet McCrickard, Gothic Image, 1990.

9- 'The Earth Goddess', Cheryl Stratton, Blandford Press, 1997.

10- 'The Book of Magic', Chronicle Books, USA.

11- 'Handbook of Irish Antiquities', William F. Wakeman, Bracken Books, London,1891.

12- 'Mysterious Britain', Janet and Colin Bord, Garnstone Press, 1972.

13- 'The Message from Water', Masaru Emoto, Ehlers Verlag, Germany, email: vertieb@ehlersverlag.de (via Dowsers Society NSW newletter, vol 13, no 1).

14- 'Sacred Dance'. Maria-Gabriele Wosien. Thames and Hudson. UK. 1974.

15- 'The Green Man'. Ronald Miller. SB Publications. UK.

16- 'Pilgrimage in Ireland.' Peter Harbison. Barrie and Jenkins. London. 1991.

4:2 Irish Round Towers

Travelling through Ireland one is amazed at the sense of timelessness, for here traditions hold strong and time has not swept away so many of the old forms. Monuments of old remain largely respected or revered, and are thus better preserved and more numerous than elsewhere in Europe.

One of the greatest curiosities to be seen are large rocket shaped Round Towers that dot the countryside, boldly emerging from amidst the ruins of monastic centres. Uniquely Irish in style, they have become a symbol of native culture – cleverly

Photo Junitta Vallak

constructed, stunningly and elegantly simple of form and often towering above all other architecture.

They also reek of mystery. For while the tourist guides will glibly state that they were bell towers and defensive structures, neither of these explanations make good sense. They made lousy safe havens during times of warfare, with many an important person plus the monastery treasures burning to smithereens inside them. And it certainly looks doubtful if bell ringing on the top floor could have been practically feasible.

Towers have always been the stuff of romantic myths and legends, where maidens were once imprisoned or kept for safekeeping and gods visited. One mythic maiden was not too safe in there though, as she was impregnated by a god from above who manifested as a golden shower of light! A visitor from Sirius perhaps? In the Arthurian legends when Merlin, who was said to be descended from a superior race, left the Earth he 'rejoined his people in the traditonal way - by entering a Tower.' [1]

Tower fascination is reinforced when we make small scale models of Irish Towers and put them out in the garden – to find that plants will germinate and grow much faster in their presence. But were Irish Towers really intended as stone antennas for harnessing paramagnetic energy from the sun, to grow the monks' crops better, as the American insect antenna expert, Professor Phil Callahan, asserts?

Or were they modern, imported ideas intuitively expressed in response to deeper and long forgotten folk traditions? Let's look at the theories, the theorists and the historical and architectural background to get a clearer picture.

What has recorded history to say?

Some 65 Round Towers in various states of decay are found scattered around 28 of Ireland's 32 counties, while another 8 are mentioned in the Annals, but no trace of them are now to be found. The ancient Annals of Ireland (which have been rewritten and edited over time) contain 63 references to Irish Round Towers, calling them 'cloicteach', or bellhouses, noting 23 events that are repeated with variations.

Mainly they record disasters that befell Towers. Storms and lightning took their toll, as well as raiding, looting and burning; sometimes by Vikings, but more often by other Irish clans. Important clergy and noblemen who died inside them are recorded, including the King of Tara, killed by another faction in 1076, and the King of Fir Manach in 1176, who was burned by his own kinsmen.

In the Annals of the Masters we find that in 1020 the "Belfry of Slaine was burned by foreigners with it full of relics and distinguished people, together with the Lector of Slaine, the crosier of the patron saint and a bell, the best of bells." The slaughterings of noblemen suggest that Towers, like churches, were regarded as places of sanctuary. Unfortunately the concept of sanctuary was often violated, particularly by the Vikings.

After the Annals, there are no further historical references to Irish Towers until the late 17th century, when antiquarians started to take an interest. There were often inaccurate and vastly exaggerated tales about the height and form of Towers.

Henry O'Brien made an interesting case for Irish Round Towers to be of Atlantean origin, in his 1834 book 'Atlantis in Ireland'. O'Brien felt that after the biblical Flood refugees from the sunken continent made their way to Ireland. Much of his theories is unsubstantiated and fairly flawed, but make for a good read. [2]

American Ignatius Donnelly published a similar theory in his book in 1882. Donnelly believed that Round Towers were proof that Atlanteans colonised Ireland. Towers are also found in Phoenicia, Sardinia, the Shetland Islands, Colorado, New Mexico, India and South America, he claims. Some of these Towers are square, but, as in their Round Tower counterparts, the doors are said to be positioned about a third of the way up. [3]

Irish legends certainly tie in with this idea. 'Fairyland', Hy-brasil'or Tir-nan-og, that great island or sunken paradise to the west where Irish souls depart to is presumably referring to Atlantis. The religious science of the Atlanteans supposedly excelled in harnessing Earth's electro-magnetic forces, to help maintain soil fertility and health for all. The biblical Flood may be referring to the flood/earthquake/meteor impact or whatever which drowned Atlantis some 10,000 years ago. There is evidence of lava flows and fossilised freshwater algae under the Atlantic Ocean going back to that era; while underwater structures such as pyramids in the Caribbean and the 23 mysterious crystal skulls, etc, have fuelled much speculation. [4]

It is also possible that some of the original cultural influence of the megalithic races who inhabited the western European seaboard came from an amphibious advanced race of beings from the Sirius star system, although this influence could have filtered through via Atlantis, the Mediterranean, Egypt or Mesopotamia.

O'Brien won great acclaim at the time his book was published, but proved an embarrassment to the establishment. Soon another Irishman, George Petrie sought to stifle his 'wacky' theories and published the first scientific study of Round Towers in 1845. Since then and through most of the 20th century there has been a surprising paucity of publications on the subject to refute the Atlantean theory.

In 1979 Professor Barrow published his book on Towers, but this also is not known for it's historical accuracy. Barrow, for instance, assigned a much greater age to the Towers, with no means of backing up his claim. From his own scientific research, begun during world war two, Phil Callahan discovered that Towers function as 'stone antennas' which are capable of collecting cosmic energies and transmitting them to soils, which then enhances plant growth. Some of Callahan's research is unfortunately derived from Barrow's work, to further confuse things.

One of Callahan's most interesting insights into the Towers is the idea that their locations, when viewed on an Irish map, supposedly mirror the positions of the constellations of the northern sky at the winter solstice, in a kind of terrestial zodiac. At night Callahan was able to measure 14.6m long cosmic radiations from the night sky above, collected by these giant wave-guide structures.

This lead him to speculate that knowledge of astronomy from Egypt went into their making. His book – 'Ancient Mysteries, Modern Visions- the magnetic life of agriculture', published in 1984, opened up a whole new field of research. Many people think that his insights are some of the greatest discoveries of the century. [5]

At the end of last century 2 more books have been added to the small handful that exist on this fascinating subject. In 1999 the architect Brian Lalor produced the most well researched and comprehensive tome yet. Lalor has photographed and described 73 towers and attempted to date them according to architectural styles. This is a logical and welcome addition to the debate and firmly fits them into the early medieval era by style alone. [6] In 2000 Roger Stalley published a small but interesting guidebook - 'Irish Round Towers' . [7]

There has never been a systematic archeological study of the Towers to fully enlighten on us on their mysteries. For each theory that has been presented to explain the Towers, there are exceptions to the rule. It seems we may just be scratching the surface in understanding them.

What is a Round Tower?

Ireland's Round Towers are an unique architectural form, while Irish missionaries and master builders were probably responsible for the 2

Irish-style towers found in Scotland and one on the Isle of Man. They ought not be confused with later round and square towers built in a rash of revivalism in the 19th century.

Of 36 Towers still standing and complete, the leaning Tower of Kilmacduagh, county Galway, is the tallest at 34m/100' (and is featured on the book cover). Forty towers are found in association with surviving ecclesiastical settlements. The rest are in isolation, but originally there would have been a monastery there, it is felt.

The Towers have a height to diameter ratio of about 4 or 5 : 1. Walls taper in from the base at a 2 to 3 degree angle. The angle of the conical roof cap is often around 45 ^{0}, corresponding to the degree of latitude, (which is related to the angle of the sun), as Callahan notes.

Being made with Roman mortar, the Towers were able to soar much higher than any building before them. They were so strongly made that one Round Tower, at Clondalkin, had a powder mill within 8m (24') of its base which exploded in 1786, destroying every other nearby structure except for the Tower. The Tower at Maghera was toppled by an earthquake, but fell and lay unbroken on the ground, looking like a gigantic canon.

Ornamentation and symbols on towers

The archaic style early Towers were mostly plain and unadorned, but for a few exceptions. Later, when the Romanesque style came in, more ornament was adopted.

Christian symbols are strangely rare on Towers and it is usually the more Celtic patterns that are evident. Several Towers are found to have the occasional pair or two of carved heads on them, as seen at Devenish. While they may have represented saints, this also carried over a long standing Celtic tradition, for the Celts greatly revered the human head as a seat of power and spirit, and they collected them in war as prizes. The Devenish Tower has a decorative frieze on the face of the cornice (comprising lozenge and s-shapes between borders) and Temple Finghin at Clonmacnoise has an unique herringbone pattern on its cap, another bit of Celtic vogue also seen on some 11th and 12th century British buildings.

One Tower has a Celtic cross, a popular pre-Christian symbol, and on another spiral volutes are found. Drumlane Tower has 2 birds carved on it, one a cock - another favourite Celtic symbol. On one Tower there is a primitive crucifixion figure, but this may also be harking back to an earlier theme of the cyclic death and resurrection of a king (or green man) figure, as was the more ancient tradition.

One Tower sports a sheela na gig, those gargoylish and sexually explicit female figures, the sight of which was thought to help the medieval people temper their carnal desires. It may more likely have originated as a good luck goddess figure however, for pilgrims actually rubbed the Sheela's displayed genitalia, says Harbison of a figure at a station at the pilgrimage centre of Ballyvourney Castle. [8] Evidence of rubbing is also evident on Sheela na gigs seen at the Dublin Museum. According to O'Brien, Ballyvourney once had a school of 'bacachs', itinerant wanderers reminiscent of fakirs, whose chanting had an 'oriental sound'. [2]

Floors and windows

The vast majority of Round Towers have their doorways high up off the ground and Lalor believes that it is only the earliest versions which had doors dangerously low. Irreverent raiders would have seen these low doored Towers as easy targets. The highest door, at Kilmacduagh, towers at 9m (27') above the ground, dispelling any notion that a ladder could have been passed up inside the Tower. Perhaps rope ladders or a wooden staircase were once used- but there is no evidence of either.

Photo- Junitta Vallak

The orientation of doors is in most cases to the east or close to it. Generally Tower doors faced the west door entrance to the main church. Callahan has measured ELF energies concentrated by ancient monuments ranging from megalithic structures to Round Towers and gothic cathedrals.

"It appears that most healing/religious structures…are facing east so that the weak energy is at the entrance and the strong energy is at the back, where the altar or healing chamber is located" he wrote. [9]

139

Inside the Tower there were once wooden floors, below the first of which lay basements of rough undressed stone. One Tower basement has a window. In the basements of the Towers at Glendalough and Kilmacduagh are unusual small horizontal stone pipe-like rectangular passages running right through the basement wall. These may have been for drainage or air vents.

The second floor of the Towers could possibly have been the most important, for there are often corbels there (projecting stones) that could have been used as hooks to hang the leather satchels which contained the monastery's special manuscripts and other treasures. Lalor refers to this as the Treasury Floor.

Six Towers have very large second floor windows, all nearly door sized, and 4 of which face east. Treasury floor windows are generally located to the left or right above the door. As this was the only decently lit level (and some floors had no window) it is entirely feasible that relics and valuables were kept here.

Generally speaking, once the window on the second floor was positioned above the door, the rest of the windows usually spiral up from there either clockwise or anticlockwise. This would have spread out the viewing for lookout purposes. But it also mimicked the style of Continental bell-towers, whose spiral staircases dictated the arrangement. Windows were fairly small and placed at floor level.

The top floor is the only other floor with distinguishing features, although most Towers have lost their top floors. Commonly here are found 4 windows facing more-or-less the cardinal directions, and also windows aligned to look over major roads or valleys.

As for being belfries, the difficulty level would have been high. Time-keeping by bell ringing was important as it ensured that the monasterys' activities ran like clockwork, and there was punishment for tardiness. Getting up to the so-called 'bell-floor' many times in the day would have been arduous, with all the ladders to climb.

There is no surviving mechanism by which bells and ropes could have been used on the original Towers, and no such bells exist. References to grand bells being destroyed in the Annals would have referred to exquisitely wrought native hand bells.

Perhaps these were rung from the doorway or treasury windows. The typical four 'bell-floor' windows may have had something to do with the bell ringing liturgical ritual, as they created the conceptual cross-form, but there are many exceptions to this arrangement. Kilmacduagh has 6 top floor windows.

Intriguingly, the vast majority of hand bells were made in the 8th -10th centuries and bell making seems to have gone out of fashion after about 900AD, just at the time that Tower building was in its zenith. Just a few are known from the 12th century. [7]

Architectural evolution

Was the Round Tower a purely imported form or is it an expression of native Irish spirituality and cosmology? Is there evidence of an evolutionary progression towards this form?

From about 10,000BC the Neolithic peoples of western Europe started to build rectilinear long barrows, also known as dolmen and cromlechs, of massive stones, timber and earth. These ceremonial monuments to the dead are some of the oldest human monuments found. Some 40,000 odd long barrows survive.

Styles changed around 3000BC, when circular monuments became the fashion. In Ireland (and also north Wales and north Scotland) such tomb shrines were built as gigantic round mounds with one or more straight passages leading to central stone chambers, such as the impressive 5000 year old passage-graves seen at Newgrange. These had stone carvings inside and were solar oriented, usually aligned to the winter solstice. [10]

Originally all important settlements were within large circular earthen embankments called ring forts. The drystone passage graves and cashels of Ireland are also circular structures. There was perhaps a sense of sacred, magical protection conveyed by the circular form. Lalor argues that the Round Tower is just a stone cashel plus Roman cement, which allowed it to soar upward, in imitation of continental belfies.

The Grianan of Aileach (Stone house of the Sun), near Londonderry, county Donegal, is the most famous antiquity in Ulster. It was a royal site occupied from about the 5th - 12th century according to Lalor, although others have assigned it far greater antiquity, while Donnelly says that Ptlomey mentions it in 140AD.

This low stone tower ('cashel'), built on the summit of a round hill 263m (802') above sea level, rises from 3 large concentric circle earth ramparts. From this central focal point one can view 5 counties, and dowsing reveals many ley lines converging on it. It's single entrance faces east, as is traditional with all ringforts (and later churches). The stone work of this important building displays all the design elements of the archaic styled Round Towers. That is – the circular design with battered walls (they incline inwards), and the doorways primitively lintelled and door jambs inclined.

A Grianan is a generic name for a stone building on a mountain top where the sun first strikes, or later a sun room on top of a house. This was traditionally an abode of women, where men were barred, and one existed at Tara. In legends these grianan were depicted as places of imprisonment, where daughters were kept away from men. It was also the throne room of matriarchal heroines. Fairy queens were said to live in grianan made from crystal – 'fairy bowers'. The Grianan of Aileach was said to be ruled by 3 'princes' - the sun, moon and stars. So it may have partly functioned as an observatory.

The cashel was wrecked in 676, then again in 1101 by the King of Munster and later 'restored', in the 19th century. It is one of the few archeological remains from the late Iron Age / early medieval era, the other such cashels from that period being Dun Aenghus, on Inishmore in the Aran islands, and Staige Fort, in county Kerry.

Other circular clues can be seen in the landscape. Stone circles and standing stones abound in Ireland. Many such megaliths still function energetically today, acting like Earth acupuncture needles. In an agrarian society the cult of fertility was meant to reinforce cyclic cultural renewal. The people appealed ritually to the forces of nature to ensure the harmonising of yin and yang energies. The phallic nature of standing stones and Towers seems well suited, if they were indeed meant to convey the yang cosmic forces into the womb of Mother Earth.

Lalor has devised a means of rough chronological dating of Towers that's based on architectural styles. This is very convincing, although he says that masonry styles are not so reliable as there is no logical progression. Irish masons were conservative and mostly stuck to old styles.

The style of the Round Towers remained constant over the 250 odd year time span that they were built over. In fact the general circular planning concept lasted longer in Ireland than anywhere else in Europe, from the late Neolithic to the late Medieval eras; having first been used for funeral and ritual, then domestic, military and ecclesiastic purposes.

Native building tradition that was static for 500 years only changed when more ornate Romanesque styles became the fashion during the 11th century. They changed totally in the 12th century when the rectilinear and orderly ways of the Normans where brought in by force.

The circular planning model is still evident around many important church centres, in the layout of houses and streets. Another feature still associated with Towers and monasteries are the processional rows of trees lining the roads that lead to these settlements.

From Bronze to Iron Age

Pagan Celtic peoples with advanced technologies poured into Ireland from around 650 - 300BC and began to displace native culture to some extent. Society didn't change too much, however, and after the Celtic invasion Ireland enjoyed a very long spell of relatively peaceful independence, until the Norman invasion began in 1169AD.

The Iron Age, that had begun with the Celtic arrivals had just ended in 432AD when St Patrick's mission began in Ireland. Over the course of the second half of the Iron Age the face of Ireland changed very rapidly, as woodland gave way to cultivated land, with the advent of new iron farming tools. This is seen in pollen records. The change was greatly accelerated in the 4th to 5th centuries, and this probably reflects the introduction of the iron plough.

Interestingly, tradition states that iron keeps away fairies and witches. An iron key placed under a chair is said to render a witch harmless. With the Iron Age came the demise of the old traditions and nature spirit lore. Iron is known by dowsers to 'interrupt' subtle energies and as the landscape was so drastically changed during the Iron Age it is easy to see why some people consider it's advent as the end of humanity's more harmonious relationship with nature.

During her years of independence, Ireland developed a culture of relative peace with surprising egalitarianism. Each of the 5 provinces were controlled by tense alliances of some 150 petty and principal dynasties, who claimed kingship of usually fairly small territories (called 'tuatha'). There may have been a total population of around 500,000 people at this time it is thought, with kinship bonds very strong. Clan groups, comprising 4 generations related to a common ancestor, lived together within their ramparted earthen enclosures, the ringforts. There much raiding and warfare between the groups. The indigenous culture, although fractured by the politics of a multitude of kingdoms, was surprisingly cohesive across the island.

A virtually national code, the Brehan laws exalted justice and bestowed on women a fairly good status. Internationally, the Irish became renowned for their wisdom and knowledge. The legal system operated despite the absence of any central administration and depended on consensus and the authority of specialist legal scholars – the Brehon- who were maintained by the local magnates.

Full legal status was determined by land and cattle ownership. Landless tenants were serfs or clients of a lord who were expected to give gifts of cattle to them. Their homes, built from timber and wattle-and-daub, wouldn't have had the protection of ringforts, so there is little trace of the habitations of the lower status folk.

Along comes St Patrick

The Christian era meant the formal end of paganism, although it never truly stamped it out. The Church was cunning enough to simply re-use pagan sites, in order to more easily gain the allegiance of the natives. The Romans had had similar pagan beliefs as the Irish, after all. Thus in AD60 Pope Gregory 1st wrote to St Augustine in Britain urging that pagan temples should not be destroyed, but sought out, purified and converted to churches. Many such churches were thus built on hill tops and associated with solar deities who were later converted to saints.

There was much resistance to the new religion in Ireland, where folk tradition is so strong. Some people consider that the so-called Celtic Church was a blending of paganism and Christianity. Many images and pagan practises were absorbed, but not as much as in Italy, Sicily and Greece. According to modern Druid Phillip Carr-Gomm the Celtic Church was actually a myth promulgated by Protestant reformists who wanted to reinstate this more 'native' religion as an alternative to Roman Catholicism. Research in the 1970's dispelled the myth of the Celtic Church, he writes. [10]

Already in 431AD Ireland's first Bishop, Palladius, was sent from Roman Britain, so there must have been a substantial Christian population by then to warrant this. St Patrick came of his own accord from Wales, prompted by a vision, and travelled mainly around the northern half of the island. The strength of Irish paganism and sun worship is evident when St Patrick told the Irish in the 5th century that "Christ is the true sun".

By those times there was obvious Roman and continental influence, with its technological advances. But nonetheless when Tower building began, some 500 years after St Patrick, the builders clung to their archaic styles – proof of the absence of any strong foreign influence.

Between the 5th and the 13th centuries, dispersed agricultural settlements amidst open grassland were numerous. Up to 50,000 ringfort settlements are known. These would have contained the tribal homesteads and the cattle, protected from wolves by fences on top of the ramparts. (Even bodies buried in graveyards were not safe from wolves!) Some ringforts were political power centres and some monastic settlements, and many of these were probably both. Each would have been self-sufficient, with skills in all crafts. The level of technology was up to that of anywhere else, with just one element missing – virtually no ceramics were made. There was a total reliance of timber.

Monasteries

In the 6th century the Irish church began to adopt ideas of monasticism from Egypt and Syria. The concept fitted very nicely with the patterns of settlement already in place.

Soon the monastic community had become the key expression of the early Irish church, whilst it upheld social continuity and order. The abbacy was a matter of family inheritance and kinship bonding. Thus the monastery founder and saints were always of noble birth or related to the ruling families.

The monastic cities were organically structured, unlike the highly organised religious orders of the continent. Buildings were small and unlit (until Towers were built), with lots of little churches and associated structures positioned higgledy piggledy.

Wooden, or even wattle and daub, churches were originally the norm, except in the west where rock was plentiful. Timber churches were all gone by the 10th century and replaced by stone ones, while less important buildings would still have been made from timber. [7]

Irish Pilgrimage Abroad

The ninth century German monk Strabo spoke of the "Irish people whom the custom of travelling to foreign lands has now become almost second nature". Irish pilgrims were known as 'peregrini' in the great age of pilgrimage to Rome and the Continent, starting around the 6th century. One can imagine the excitement and adventure afforded by going on pilgrimage, which must have been an expensive exercise and exclusive to the upper echelons only. Kings and upper-class clergy were the original Irish tourists.

There were well organised pilgrimage routes, with special Irish hostels provided for them. Irish bishops would often ordain people as priests on their journeys and Irish scholars were working in the Carolingian courts. The continental secular authorities became unhappy with the Irish pilgrims' behaviour and by the 8th century they had become persona non grata in foreign lands and were being encouraged to make their pilgrimages back home in Ireland.

Wealthy pilgrims in their wanderings would have looked at wonder at the ecclesiastical buildings of the Carolingian empire (in France, Germany and Belgium) and noted with envy the shapes of buildings, such as belfries, never seen in Ireland. The scale of building on the continent was vastly bigger than in Ireland and must have been awe-inspiring to the Irish. Italian Campanile towers were present at the major centres of continental pilgrimage, in Rome, Ravenna and other places. Pilgrims must have decided that they too had to have these towering status symbols for their monasteries at home. [8]

Spiritual reforms in Ireland brought in by the Culdee movement around 800AD discouraged international pilgrimage and some people have attributed Tower building to their initiatives. The Culdees have also been associated with the Druids.

Age of the Round Tower

From the 8th century Ireland's own pilgrimage centres began to spring up everywhere, with Towers possibly starting to be built from this time (some think from the 10th century). The continental belfries would have been emulated at home by local stonemasons who were only conversant with vernacular archaic architectural styles. They were able to adapt the Iron Age cashel form thanks to the great new innovation of Roman cement, and thus Towers soared skywards. Towers provided a grand landmark for pilgrims to see from afar, a lookout if trouble came, a treasury, as well as a place to routinely ring hand bells from.

Towers went up in the churchyard enclosure at various distances from the church, and were typically oriented to the left or right of the west door of the original church, that is – to its north-west or south-west. There was little other planning at the monastic settlements and churches were added ad hoc, aligned east-west so that their altar end faced Jerusalem. Only the Round Tower seemed to be in a special spatial relationship with the main church.

It could well be that this preferred location was in direct mimicry of the continental habit of having the belfry as one of a collection of architectural features known as 'westwork'. Carolingian Towers were built to the west of the church between the 8th and 10th centuries. Unlike the Irish Towers also built around that time, those bell towers were 'engaged', that is attached to other structures or each other. [6]

There was obviously a logical purpose for the Irish juxtaposition, which must have been purely practical, in that the congregation could not fit inside the tiny churches and would have gathered around the high crosses outside and next to the Tower, from where they could see the goings on at the doors of both church and Tower.

The Irish Pilgrimage

The new focus on pilgrimage within Ireland incorporated many original pagan practises and one wonders what relevance it had to Christian worship. Fortunately it preserved many fascinating folk customs. Pagan gods were simply renamed and a veneer of Christianity applied to native festivities that celebrated the cyclic bounty of nature, and paid homage to the fertilising forces of nature, and the healing powers of water and stone.

For instance the important pilgrimage practices at Mt Brandon were a muted echo of previous activities which celebrated the local harvest god Crom Dubh on Crom Dubh Sunday, the last Sunday in July. The pilgrimage involved a night climb vigil, prayers at a ruined oratory on the summit, which was then encircled by pilgrims, and thence off to ancient mounds and a pillar stone called the Stone of the Backs. You stood with your back against this pillar for a backache cure. After climbing the summit it was the practise to go back to the village of Cloghane for games, athletics, horse vaulting, dancing, singing, feasting and courtship. The Catholic clerics tried to purge this merriment in the 18th century. In 1868 a Bishop tried to revive the tradition, but it had died out.

A similar 4 day revelry occurred annually at Glendalough - that most important of learning centres, south of Dublin. A reputation for rowdiness, drunkedness and the odd faction fight caused the Catholic church to ban pilgrimage there in 1862. It is one of the few pilgrimage sites which has a well defined pilgrimage road leading to it, from west Wicklow and over the Wicklow gap. Around the beginning of this route near Hollywood a granite stone with a labyrinth carving was found (on right, Dublin Museum).

The Church also banned pilgrimage from Inishcealtra, county Clare, on an island in the lower Shannon, where legends speak of a sacred tree. The patron saint's feast day celebrations, held at the Lady Well, happened to coincide with the Celtic god Lugh's harvest festival. A 24m (75') high Round Tower stands there. The ban was enacted when the Chuch got tired of the local boys carrying off young maidens for

'greenwood' marriages, as was the old custom, which, they lamented, no law could stop them from doing.

At a pilgrimage centre at Inishmurray, off the Sligo coast, pilgrims visited the holy well of St Molais and then a number of rounded stones called the 'cursing stones', some of which had had crosses carved on them for a veneer of respectability! These stones are one of the most celebrated features on the island. The obviously pagan tradition was to make curses by first fasting, then walking around the spot widdershins, turning the stones 3 times and unleashing one's curse each time. If the curse was unjustified it would recoil back to the curser. In world war two Hitler was cursed at this place. Nearby at a large upright stone with holes at its corners it has been customary for expectant mothers to put their fingers through these holes to ensure successful childbirth.

Another curious feature at pilgrimage and monastic sites are ancient ceremonial stones called bullauns which have up to 9 bowl like depressions carved into them. These are sometimes associated with cures, such as removing warts. Less commonly, the rounded stones kept in some bullaun hollows were used as cursing stones, turned around to effect a curse, says Harbison. It has been suggested that water held in the hollows might once have been used to 'capture' the sun's rays on special days, so they could have been used as simple radionic devices for remedy making and curse broadcasting.

Pilgrimage at Glencolmcille, county Donegal, started at the Protestant chapel, from where people proceeded barefoot to the first station - a megalithic mound, where they kneeled and prayed. At the second station a decorated pillar stone is walked around 3 times and prayers said, kneeling again. At the third station one kneels on a stone cairn with special knee hollows, then the pilgrim picks up a rounded stone, blesses themselves with it, passes it over to the back of the body and around to the front three times.

At the next station - St Colmcille's chapel, is a long flagstone known as St Colmcille's bed, where one lies down, turns 3 times and then puts their left hand down to take a little earth from under the bed. This is kept as a protection against fire and as a cure for headaches and other ailments. Clay is also removed from under a large stone with a cross on top and this is said to grant requests.

At the important monastic city of Clonmacnoise, in the centre of the country, from where a beautiful gold torc from circa 3000BC was once unearthed, pilgrims made their way to the tombshrine of founder St Ciaran and took a little clay soil from there to carry home and steep in water to drink, as a 'sovereign remedy against diseases of all sorts'. The Round Tower there is almost, but not exactly, in a direct line with the Pilgrim's Way, as it approaches St Ciaran's tomb shrine. Clonmacnoise is positioned beneath Polaris, the north pole star, on the star map of the northern sky.

Use of earth from a saint's grave to obtain cures was also widely practised across Europe and beyond in the early years of Christianity. Bells and other relics often had cures and miracles associated with them too. [8] So relics were important drawcards for the many centres of pilgrimage and it is easy to imagine the relic-envy that might have spawned the raiding of monasteries, as a continuation of the rivalry and warfare that had always existed between the various clans.

One can also imagine the souvenir hungry pilgrims soon depleting the reserves of soil and clay at these points. It is no wonder then that some buildings at pilgrimage centres had barricades built to keep people out, and that the Round Tower doors were high up, to keep out the curious masses and miracle seekers, and to safely display the housed relics to the pilgrims below.

Fire Temples?

O'Brien thought that some Round Towers may have been connected with sacred fire worship. He noted that the Venerable Bede, mentioned in the Life of St Cuthbert, complained that there were numerous fire receptacles, remaining from pagan times, still existing in Ireland. The remains of low stone-roofed 'firehouses', similar to Persian ones, are associated with Towers at Ardmore, Killaloe, Down, Kerry and Kells, he wrote. [2] The Round Tower adjacent to the cathedral at Brechin in Scotland is known as the 'fire tower'. [11]

The fire temple may well have been amongst the earliest sacred structures within the Irish ringfort settlements. At Inishmurray, central to its ecclestiastical remains, is a great drystone cashel covering about one third of an acre, with internal low walled subdivisions. Two stone and mortar churches date from 7-900AD, while the outer wall is probably Iron Age. In the western corner of the cashel are 2 buildings, one a church and one a 'House of Fire' which could be late medieval, according to Peter Harbison.

There is an entrance in both of the long sides of this rectangular building with a square hearth in the centre. In tradition a fire was kept permanently burning there. Nearby are famous 'cursing stones', ancient beehive huts (stone huts) and a sweat house close to a holy well. [8]

Almost to modern times ancient worship of the goddess Brigid/St Brigid continued at her sacred women-only shrine in Kildare, near to the Round Tower there. Nineteen 'vestal' virgins tended an undying fire, while on the 20th day of the cycle the fire was said to be miraculously tended by Brigid herself.

Into the 18th century an ancient song was sung to this lingering goddess – "Brigid, excellent woman, sudden flame, may the bright fiery sun take us to the lasting kingdom".

Norman conquest

During their heyday Towers suffered all sorts of injustice, noted in the Annals, thanks to the greed of the neighbouring lords plus the odd Viking raid. The difference between being attacked by the Irish and Vikings was that the Vikings did not observe the concept of sanctuary that had become associated with monasteries, although the Irish frequently abused this concept also. The adherence to the rules of combat and social order in Ireland would have perhaps deemed the Towers as useful safehouses in warfare, until this was put to the test many times and failed miserably.

After the Normans were invited to bring in their mercenaries to bolster a local king's fight over his stolen wife in 1169, it was the beginning of the end to organic social planning and autonomy. The highly ordered world of the Normans, characterised by rectilinear building principles, usurped the organic, curvilinear mode of the native Irish and ushered in 800 odd years of Irish repression by the English. The natives were driven from their fertile lands and left to fend for themselves in more inhospitable regions. No more Towers were built from then on.

In the 1840's a devastating potato blight wiped out possibly 800,000 people, with many more emigrating to America and Australia. The English colonists did little to help as the Irish starved to death. The population, up to about 9 million at the time, fell to around 6.5 million by 1851 (and is lesser nowadays.) An independent Irish republic in the south was not achieved until 1949.

The English had suppressed the Irish language and even basic education, so it was no wonder that they were regarded as stupid, and became the butt of Irish jokes. When Ken Livingstone, a thorn in English Prime Minister Margaret Thatcher's side, assumed his enlightened control of the Greater London Council in the late 1970's one of his first actions was to ban Irish jokes from within the city.

The English repeated this cultural genocide in Australia, and justified their invasion, which broke their own laws, by saying that the Aboriginals were merely an inferior race, doomed to die out, which, of course, their genocidal activities were hastening.

Tower revival

In the 18th century Irish nationalism was on the rise and the people romanticised the uniquely Irish Tower as quinessentially theirs. Seen as national symbols, along with Irish wolfhounds and harps, Towers began

Musk Tower and late medieval add-ons.

to be built all over Ireland in imitation. By the 19th century many of the original surviving Towers had also been pressed into service again and rebuilt or 'restored' by the Anglican church. They were fitted out with floors and ladders and the tops redesigned to make proper belfries. Often the caps had been blown off by lightning, so we'll never know their original form. Lightning had been the biggest threat to Towers in all their existence, for being located over underground springs meant that lightning was highly attracted. The 19th century make-overs included fitting lightning rods, which was a great boon.

No more were returned to use after disestablishment of the church in 1871. [7]

What Towers were probably not

Some of Callahan's ideas about Towers are derived from Barrow's book that, according to Lalor, is an untrustworthy source of information. Barrow had stated that piles of dirt had been used to fill up the space between the first floor and the ground level of the Towers. Callahan had deduced that this was the monks' means of tuning these stone 'antennae' to certain radio-wave frequencies from space.

At no Tower in Ireland have I seen evidence of this and certainly there is quite the opposite indication from the architectural surveys in Lalor's book. In fact empty basements are common, and one even has its own window, although there is nothing to say that the basements might have been

153

excavated by treasure seekers long ago.

In the book 'Secrets of the Soil' the chapter on Callahan's discoveries in relation to Irish Towers begins with the statement that windows of the old Towers were oriented to cast shadows to indicate the quarter days of the year. I also find no evidence to back this one up.

There is no proof of especially good plant growth around Towers, as in Callahan's supposition. Towers today tend to be found within graveyards, with some graves butting right up to them. In fact there is evidence, says Lalor, that graves were pre-existing at sites where Towers were built. Photos of Towers I have not visited often show bleak and hostile surrounds. One finds it hard to believe that gardening went on within the ecclesiastical compound.

So there is no conclusive evidence that Towers were deliberately built to improve the growth of crops, as Callahan contends. I suspect that there is plenty of hype getting around about them. But that doesn't negate the fact that Towers old and new have energetic effects which we can duplicate in our own backyards.

As for the bell-tower concept, they may well have been intended as bell-towers, but the Irish hand bells seem to have gone out of fashion just as Towers were starting to be built. So perhaps their role of being the monastery treasury was a more important Tower function.

Conjecture

I can see nothing to suggest that monasteries were deliberately building Towers as 'stone age radio receivers', as Callahan asserts, however their locations, which equate to a 'terrestial zodiac', are certainly intriguing. However I suggest that this was because they were coincident with the ancient pre-Christian centres of learning.

The important learning centres, the original universities, were where a great many cultural advances and intellectual developments were fostered. The Druid schools were very much concerned with astronomy and hence this must have carried over by default. The 4 quarters were sacred to the Druids and this might have helped dictate door and window orientation. It is highly probable that lingering traditions also dictated careful geomantic placement at a site, or that people instinctively or intuitively chose high energy points to build the Towers on, knowing that extra sanctity would then be afforded them. Folk memories of standing stones and stone circles which possibly were previously present there could have also been used as placement criteria.

The effects of the Tower energies as found by Callahan are stimulating of consciousness, mental activity and creativity. They would have heightened spiritual experiences, just as Earth energies associated with churches would have done.

So I think that the enigma of the Round Tower can be explained as a case of intuitive planning, of an adherence to pagan principles in a resurgance of subconscious memory of ancient understandings.

References:

1- 'The Flying Saucer Vision', John Michell, Abacus, UK, 1974.
2- 'Atlantis in Ireland - the Round Towers of Ireland', Henry O'Brien, original –1834, Steiner Books, USA, 1976.
3- 'Atlantis- the Antediluvian World', Ignatius Donnelly, Steinerbooks, originally published in 1882.
4- 'Atlantean Tradition in Ancient Britain', Anthony Roberts, Rider and Co, UK, 1975.
5- 'Ancient Mysteries, Modern Visions – the Magnetic Life of Agriculture' Phil Callahan, Acres USA, 1984.
6- 'The Irish Round Tower, origins and architecture explored', Brian Lalor, The Collins Press, 1999.
7- 'Irish Round Towers, Roger Stalley, Country House, Dublin 2000.
8- 'Pilgrimage in Ireland, the monuments and the people', Peter Harbison, Barrie and Jenkins, London. 1991.
9- 'Paramagnetism', Philip S. Callahan, Acres USA, 1995.
10- 'Druid Renaissance', Phillip Carr-Gomm, UK.
11- 'Mysterious Britain'. Janet and Colin Bord, Garnstone Press. 1972.

4.3 Dowsing the Round Towers

From my dowsing survey of 16 Irish Towers in April 2000 I have come to suspect that the Towers were placed over previously holy sites. Perhaps there once stood a megalith or stone circle, marking an Earth acupuncture point where Heaven on Earth was celebrated by ancient pagans, their rituals aiming to enhance regional prosperity and fertility.

This I've surmised by the presence of strong energy patterns that are dowsable at all the old Towers. More recent Towers do not usually have dowsable energies beneath them.

Irish-Australian dowser Sanderson Griffin described the dowsing pattern at Irish Towers, when he returned from surveying 10 of them, in May 2000. He likened the view from above as " - if you could see the water, it would be like looking at a Celtic cross pattern". The Round Tower superimposed by the equal armed cross, being 4 underground streams emanating from a central spring (also known as a 'source', 'water dome' or 'blind spring').

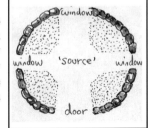

Sandy found that the 4 underground streams beneath the 10 Towers were mostly at least 1m (3') wide, the strongest stream being directly beneath the doorway. This correlated with my dowsing survey, the both of us finding that the widest / strongest stream was not only always at the doorway, but the same width as it too.

Most underground streams that I dowsed, which were not always in fours, corresponded with the positions of the windows, or what remained of windows. Perhaps this was the reason why windows don't always match the cardinal directions?

Crossings of underground streams and water domes have a secondary dowsable pattern associated with them, being a downward yin energy vortex, which also spirals up the Tower. This effect is also seen at standing stones, and dowsers such as Tom Graves have written of their dowsing experiences with them (- more about this in 4.5).

Callahan also found bands of energy to manifest in the deposition of Epsom salt crystals, in an experiment with miniature cardboard models of Towers. He believes that these concentrated salt bands corresponded with the intense energies where floor, door and window levels of Towers are located. They could well be describing the path of the vortex.

Energy parallels elsewhere

The water connection comes as no surprise, considering the strong correlation between underground water and other antiquities. Back in 1939 the British Society of Dowsers published an article by a famous archeologist Reginald Smith, describing how he had divined so-called 'blind springs' in the centre of ancient structures in England, such as the Rollright stone circle, at ring forts, Stonehenge, in front of church altars, etc. These energy flows respond to the varying phases of the moon, he found. From more recent archeological studies, it is thought that an important calendrical function of stone circles was probably for lunar eclipse predictions.

Smith concluded that "the constant presence of underground water at the exact centre of these earthworks and circles is a significant feature easily verifiable by others in the field." In the1940's dowser Guy Underwood confirmed many of these findings (see water lines he dowsed on barrows below), although he stated that "Reg Smith refers to certain complexes of underground streams as 'blind springs' (but) I am inclined to think that

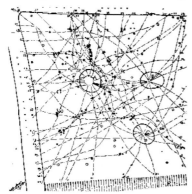

some of them must be merely multiple intersecting fissures. The name 'blind spring' is, however, convenient."

English churches share this type of locational criteria, not surprisingly, as they often usurped an older pagan temple. Underwood found that water lines coincided with the dimensions and shape of church buildings, with the strongest spring often located directly beneath the church tower, where "the celestial influences attracted by the spire combined with the terrestial force to produce an energy fusion", as would have been the purpose of earlier pagan activities.

Likewise Muriel Langdon, in another early BSD Journal article describes dowsing water lines at churches. "Water domes are like spokes of a wheel, with some flowing in and some out. Water lines run up the centre of the nave and chancel and another runs across from the north to south doors. Domes are found at altars, at the centre of the chancel steps, the font and at all doors," she found, noting that primitive Welsh churches are not associated with water at all. [2]

The altar is the focal point in most Christian churches, either being in the centre or at the eastern end. It has long been infused with religious mystery and the area around it is often reserved solely for the clergy. Its form ranges from a simple wooden table with a cross above or on it, up to the most ornately carved or jewel encrusted altar. It is also the focal point for Eucharist celebrations (thanksgiving in Greek). [3] When Vikings plundered Clonmacnoise, their leader Turgeis's wife Ota is recorded as giving oracles on the church altar there.

Guy Underwood, in 'The Pattern of the Past' noted that gnats are often seen to be swarming around church spires and that they are known to 'dance' above blind springs, with which the spires are associated. Also - yew trees, poisonous to livestock but sacred to the medieval church and Druid tradition, are said to grow best over 'blind springs.' Perhaps this helps explain their presence in the ruins of monastic sites. [4]

Early Irish builders requiring guidance on sighting their sacred structures, had the tradition of sending out dun cows - of great mystical significance, which led the people to geomantically correct sites. Cows tend to be attracted to the same types of energies us humans revere.

Not surprisingly I discovered this for myself when advising on Tower locations one day. I was visiting Ron and Bev Smith's Gippsland dairy farm and arrived in the evening. Before actually seeing the farm I began to do some map dowsing that evening, to locate possible positions for Towers. Ron, who is very closely connected to his land and animals, had a bit of a chuckle because all of the locations I found turned out to be favourite spots where the cows congregated.

Why Water?

The energy that emanates from underground water domes and water-courses can be very unhealthy to live over. There are found to be concentrations of positive ions, microwaves and other intense radiations at the geopathic zones, which are best avoided, if possible. (However insects and micro-organisms thrive there.)

But, following the principles of homeopathy, we find that a short dose of this water energy is stimulating and can help people attain altered states of consciousness. Thus the ancients must have sought it out to boost their psycho-spiritual experiences. Likewise, normally taboo areas in Australian Aboriginal lore, such as uranium orebody areas, where is it unhealthy to spend too long, may be visited for short spells for ceremonial activity.

Water attracting Towers?

If the powerful geomantic locations where we find Towers was not deliberate, then there is always the possibility that the Round Towers 'attracted' the water energies and vortex to themselves. There has always been the chicken-and-egg debate in geomantic discussions on what came first- the structure (temple, standing stone etc) or the Earth energies associated with it. Sacred structures can become highly energetic from the activities of the people using them and even modern structures can attract ley line energy to them.

This phenomena has been noted in relation to modern labyrinth building by John Wayne Blassingame, a speaker at the American Society of Dowsers West Coast Conference in 1999. When a labyrinth has been put in place it is found by Blassingame to have attracted water to underneath it, in the form of a water dome.

A long time well dowser, he is certain that there was no water in the vicinity of his own labyrinth before construction, and has been drilling in the area to prove his dowsing findings. [6]

When Sandy Griffin dowsed a relatively modern small Round Tower, built as a church belfry in the 1800's, he was amazed to find indications of a 'source' beneath it too. Was this accidental or do the Towers really attract water to them from both above and below?

I was surprised to dowse a water line crossing at the Irish Turoe Stone, a ceremonial stone with approximately 2000 year old La Tene style decorative carving on it's top.

Not that this is not the norm with ancient megaliths. But after my dowsing I was told by the land owner that this stone was moved from its former position to its current location some 150 years ago. Perhaps the person who moved it was a dowser? Or the stone attracted the water? (I dreamt that night of hovering above the Turoe Stone and watching a stream of energy emanating upwards from its peak.)

It is thus quite possible that Towers were placed more randomly than supposed and that their form or the forces channelled to Earth by them were in some degree responsible for a 'water raising force', as Graefe described the effect of his 'humus medicine'. They may have energetically attracted a spring to them.

Ley lines

Sandy also found Round Towers to be often associated with ley lines, which cross usually directly above the Tower. Ley lines are yang, linear energy paths in the air, that also engage with Earth energy points. Some call them 'overgrounds', 'dreaming tracks' or 'song lines', etc. Originally they referred more to alignments of ancient structures in the landscape, as discovered by Alfred Watkins.

They are known by dowsers (some of whom call them 'energy leys') to reflect patterns of human activity and thought, and they will manifest at sacred sites and civic centres alike, wherever there is a focus of human consciousness.

Some people consider leys as huge thought lines of consciousness and certainly they have been used to spread ideas and even evil propaganda. Hitler employed geomancers to use the ancient sacred sites network to conduct magical rituals that would help him gain and hold power. He stole the swastika, which is a global solar symbol, for his own powermongering as well.

In Britain and Ireland ley lines are associated mostly with structures and alignments. Nichols mentions important alignments of sacred centres in Ireland which include Towers. "Tailtown…is exactly on the line of latitude

160

with New Grange and there is a straight orientation to the north-east from Tara to Knowth and the Round Tower near Monasterboice. New Grange, Knowth and Dowth form a triangle pointing north-east" he writes.[5]

Paramagnetic energy fields

Tuning to the paramagnetic energy fields emanating from the Towers themselves made my pendulum do characteristic helicopter gyrations. According to Sandy these energy fields varied a lot in size, from a radius of only a few metres (yards) to about 100m (100 yds) across. They certainly were not as strong or extensive as we might have expected.

Nonetheless the monks (or were they Druids in disguise?) would have experienced the powerful ley line energies as they sat, chanting perhaps, on various Round Tower levels. Together with the spiralling energy vortex of the underground spring and the intense paramagnetic field of the Tower itself, this potent energy cocktail, I would think, must have ably facilitated the altered states of consciousness and exalted religious experience that they craved.

The Tower builders must have been most pleased with their architectural efforts, as the vitalising energies within and around them would have stimulated much intellectual development and religious piety.

References:

1- 'Needles of Stone', Tom Graves, Turnstone Books, UK, 1978.
2- 'Dowsing and Archeology', editor Tom Graves, British Society of Dowsers, 1980.
3- 'World Religions' by Duncan Baird Publishers, London, 1998.
4- 'The Pattern of the Past'. Guy Underwood. Pitman, UK. 1969.
5- 'The Book of Druidry'. Ross Nichols, Thorsons, London. 1990.
6- Dowsers Society of NSW newsletter vol 11, no 9.

4:4 *Towers of Power*

Callahan 's perspectives

Professor Phil Callahan PhD (born 1923) began to investigate the Irish Round Towers when he was stationed near one during world war two. He observed farmers ferry their cows in row boats to Devenish Island so they could enjoy the lush grass around the Tower there, and he began to suspect that there might be a connection between it and the good growth.

From his discoveries about paramagnetism, Callahan found that 25 of the Round Towers are made from limestone that is, unusually, paramagnetic (from the presence of clay), 13 are of red, paramagnetic sandstone, and the rest are made of basalt, clay slate and granite, all of which are also paramagnetic. The stone used in their construction was not always the local rock, for only paramagnetic rock was selected.

On the other hand Irish dwellings, he found, were always constructed of diamagnetic rock, such as limestone, and this would have provided a more relaxed atmosphere to live in.

Callahan feels that the Egyptians were able to distinguish between the paramagnetic and diamagnetic energies inherent in stone. They had two hieroglyphic symbols for stone, both rectangles, one with stripes (a "wave pattern"), perhaps to signify paramagnetic rock. Callahan thinks that the Egyptians may have passed on their masonry skills to the Irish. Towers at Devenish and Clonmacnoise have herringbone type patterns on their caps, which Callahan says may be mimicking the energy wave patterns.

Constructed as they are of paramagnetic stone and shaped as giant waveguides, the Round Towers act as magnetic antennae, drawing down energies beneficial to soil, he says. Callahan is well known for his studies of insect antennae, and calls Towers "massive electronic collectors of cosmic microwave energy" as well as "giant accumulators of magnetic energy".

By day Towers resonate to the magnetic energy from the sun (collecting south pole/positive magnetic monopoles), and by night to mysterious 14.6m (48') wavelength radio-waves from the part of the sky that they were aligned to, he says. They also collect other extra-low-frequency radiations (ELF) from the cosmos and from lightning, such as Schumann resonance.

Did the ancients have antenna envy?

Vital to our health, ELF waves are able to penetrate water and soil, unlike higher frequencies of radiation. Callahan refers to Schumann waves as atmospheric brain waves, because of the shared frequencies with our own brain waves. The 8HZ and 2000Hz waves he detected at the Towers were strongest at sunrise and sunset. Energies trickle out from the Towers to vitalize the surrounding soil.

To amplify incoming ELF radiation, Towers must be paramagnetic, and the effect is enhanced even more so when paramagnetic and diamagnetic materials are sandwiched together, like the orgone accumulators of Wilhelm Reich. The wooden floors of the Irish Towers provided the diamagnetic component for the task. Sunlight amplifies Schumann waves and so does the wind. So it was no wonder to Callahan that Towers were designed to have maxiumum sun and wind exposure, with windows often facing the wind directions. He found that doors are located where Schumann resonance is strongest.

Callahan says that fence lines, power lines and underground streams also conduct Schumann resonance. A good reason for the ancients to locate their sacred sites, plus the Irish Towers, over underground water.

Callahan began to experiment with small scale models of these Towers and had enhanced plant growth when seeds were germinated in their presence. The carborundum sandpaper he used in their construction is a man made crystal of silica carbide, which happens to be an excellent semi-conductor. The mini-Towers were also soaked in a solution of diamagnetic Epsom salts for 48 hours and then dried. Patterns became apparent in the dried salt residue on these Towers, showing bands of concentrated salt occurring where window, door and floor positions are located on the real Towers. So the monks would have gained the maximum benefit of the energies as they sat on the floor.

He concluded that Towers, in their star map locations, are collectively a "huge resonant system for collecting, storing and relaying cosmic energies." [1]

Experiments with Mini Towers

When Bill Nicholson, of Geelong, Victoria experimented with a mini Tower in a plastic pot with radish plants he got startling results. "I started with two identical plastic pots filled with potting mix from the same batch," he wrote in Geomantica.

Bill made a mini Tower from a shrub branch, 40mm (2") diameter and 190mm (8") long, that was covered with sandpaper around the top 120mm (5"), with a sandpaper conical hat on top. This was inserted into one pot, buried into the potting mix to a depth of 70mm (3").

"In each pot 4 radish seeds were planted 6mm (1/4") deep at each of the compass points, that is, 4 seeds each to the north, south, east and west quarters of the pots. Watering was identical for each pot. The only differences were the presence of the Tower in one and a corresponding reduction in total volume of potting mix due to the volume of the Tower base inserted into the mix.

The 2 pots were spaced 2m (8') apart in the garden in full sun. Resulting plant growth was photographed both in the pot and later when plants were removed. Plants were pulled out of their pots in the bundles of 4, roots and all. The roots entrapped potting mix in proportion to their growth, so the weight of each plant batch and soil was an indication of root growth. After photographing, the plants were weighed. The resulting gram weights were:

Compass Point	N	E	W	S
Control Pot (g)	did not grow	7.5	12.5	25
Tower Pot (g)	20	85	62.5	55

Modern Day Towers of Power

It was John Quackenboss of Arkansas, who started the first large scale field trial of Callahan's ideas. In 1986 he erected a 1.8m (6') high terracotta pipe of 30cm (12") diameter and filled it with basalt gravel. Five pipes were spread around his 440 hectare (1,000 acre) farm. He capped them with a cone of concrete, made with basalt gravel and coated in crushed basalt, bringing the total height to 2m (8'). After 6 weeks good effects were observed. The farm enjoyed increased crop yields, despite drought conditions.

Quackenboss's Towers were positioned over the intersection of underground streams or negative intersections of the Earth's magnetic field pattern, known as the Hartman grid. He recommends 3 Towers be placed in a triangular arrangement in a field. However South Australian dowser Juergen Schmidt believes that a square or rectangular arrangement would be better in the long run, according to the rules of feng shui. The location and arrangement of Towers are probably best made individually by a competent dowser. [2]

Towers in Australia

This experimental technology appears to have created a range of interesting and beneficial effects here in Australia, judging by the feedback I have gained from supervising the building of over 50 of them since 1993. Many people have reported wonderful growth of gardens and crops. Others have reported nothing much, but they were usually the ones who hadn't put much effort into the garden anyway, or who had had bad weather.

Wooster Tower

Clarrie Wooster was possibly the first person to construct a modern Tower in Australia (in Fryerstown, central Victoria). Clarrie and family had moved there in 1989. Garden soil being poor sandstone and shale, there was nothing much growing there. After it had been devastated by a bushfire he totally re-built the garden upon feng shui lines, having traced, by dowsing, all the Earth dragon energy lines that flowed across the property. Garden beds were then constructed along these energy pathways, in curving patterns, and all plants located according to dowsing.

Wooster then decided that a Tower of Power would help, so he selected materials and a good location, by dowsing for a high energy intersection or energy line point, and started work on the Tower in July 1993. He chose to build with sandstone as it was plentiful and slightly paramagnetic. A solid tapering stone structure was erected with proper foundations and rising to 2m (8') above ground. It has an inner cavity which he filled with alternating layers of charcoal and dolomite, which were useful substances for improving his soil and might have a homeopathic effect there.

A crystal was placed at the top, over which a copper cone was positioned, giving a total height of 4m (13'). In August, a couple of weeks after the Tower was finished, the family started to notice changes in the nearby vegetable garden. Parsley growing in a very poor part of the garden and usually bitter was undoubtably sweeter than before. As spring came along and leaves burst forth they noticed a definite bluish tinge in trees and vegetables, which had never been seen before there. The broccoli was particularly good, with harvest lasting over 4 or 5 months from the same plants and not a caterpillar or cabbage moth in sight, which was very unusual.

Visitors are able to sense energy coming off the Tower, especially when a breeze is blowing, if they place the palms of their hands towards the Tower a short distance away from it. Kangaroo visits are common too. "The whole garden had an extra vibrancy" Clarrie says "and there is a sense of restfulness and peace here." [3]

Prof Callahan visited the newly built Tower when he toured Australia in August '93. He spent a few hours with his oscilloscope taking readings around the garden and said it was the "strongest Tower he had measured outside of Ireland, as strong as some of the Irish Towers despite its much smaller size."

Blooming growth

In Rye, on Victoria's Mornington Peninsula Lee Grey had a Tower erected in a part of her small vineyard that had never prospered before and where even the grass had never grown well. Nobody had ever liked to go into that area. I had been concerned that the metal wires criss-crossing the vineyard might interfere with the Tower's energy field, but this was allayed when I visited there 6 months after it went up. I talked to the WWOOFers (willing workers on organic farms) Gary and Sue, who had just been pruning the vines. There had been so much to prune in the Tower's vicinity, they said.

It was now the lushest part of the vineyard! The grass was very thick too and Lee had never seen it so good in her 5 years there. Gary and Sue had felt very good when working around the Tower and had sensed a certain warmth coming from it.

Dowsing the energy field of Lee's Tower I found it filled the whole 2.2ha (5 acre) property, then ran down the bitumen driveway and off down the road. So I wasn't surprised to hear later that when she decided to sell up, a neighbour from down this road had immediately come and bought it, much quicker than other properties were selling.

Towers are said to make for very upward growth in plants and this was most apparent after a Tower went up in the Bellingen area of NSW. Sophia was watering the plants around the Tower the next morning and found the tomato plants, which usually sprawled around the garden, were now all very upright.

Jose Robinson, a rural writer, put up a Tower on her property at Wild Cattle Island in 1997. She had been gardening there for around 20 years and had had an amazing increase in growth with the Tower. She said that the tomatoes were super abundant, "like they were going out of fashion".

After I had put up my first Tower in March 1995 on my northern NSW property I didn't notice any effect, because I had abandoned the garden in that particular poultry yard. There had been several years of drought and growing things was not worth the struggle. The area was a sea of fences, as I was breeding rare poultry, and this meant there could only be an isolated effect, or so I thought.

However I did notice that a swamp banksia tree, beyond several fences, began to change its blooming habit. Instead of putting out single flower cones, it started to sprout multiple ones, up to half a dozen in one place. No other swamp banksia was behaving this way. As you could see the Tower at a short distance away from it, I could only assume that there was an atmospheric effect going out from it, which was unexpected.

I put up 3 more Towers on the 2.2 ha (5 ac) property and experienced exponential growth, although this was partly due to the ending of the drought, with good rains in the last few years of the nineties, plus regular mulching and animal manuring. The vegetables near one Tower had never

167

My tastiest ever veges grew near a Tower.

been so lush, tasty and insect free. I would wander around the vegetable patch and eat them straight from the plants. Kids loved to eat them too. That particular garden bed also had quartz crystals, 'programmed' for good growth, at the ends of each garden row.

But the 4 Towers became a bit too much energy wise and relaxing was difficult. With all that growth, there was little time to relax anyway. One had to keep the jungle from the door! I eventually sold up and took my painted Python Tower with me to central Victoria.

General effects

Ellen and Ray Stanyer of Maldon, Victoria, have enjoyed fabulous growth on degraded soils and other effects since their Tower went up. In spring 1999 Ellen wrote to Geomantica:

"One can say it is coincident that I had to remove many, many barrow loads of weeds from the surrounds of the Tower; or that we had an incredible influx of birds; that things in our life suddenly gelled and started to happen; that money came in and not only went out…that we are so full of wonderful creative energy; well – it could be absolutely a total coincidence…

I made a mini Tower and put it amongst my poorly looking broadbeans and BOOM!! Also my clients for massage are getting more and more. I must be doing something right. Or can I put that one on the Tower too?"

Ellen and Ray's prospering young pear tree.

Lesley Gentilin, of South Australia, told me of general improvements that happened in the family after 3 PVC Towers went in. She said that before then health problems had caused her to take 6 months off work, causing much frustration. Then one day Dean "got hyperactive and put up the 3 Towers".

From them on life started to improve and she started to get her life back on track. She got back to the job that she loved, with music, and her creativity levels started to soar. The whole energy of the farm, she sensed, had changed and lots of people started to visit. She was feeling much more positive and the children's health became very good.

You don't always get what you expect with a Tower. Cherise Haslam reported that some plants suddenly died after her 2 small suburban Terracotta Pot Towers went in. But in retrospect, she said, those plants were unsuitable for the area and may well have died anyway. She did enjoy immense growth with other plants and the changed energy.

The garden felt more welcoming and she started to spend more time there. The chooks seemed to be more 'human-friendly' she said and other people commented that the garden 'felt better'.

Later she was trying to get rid of the rampant couch grass that had taken off around the Tower in the front yard. Even spraying poison on it, however, would not work. The Tower couch refused to die!

Glad Albert of western Victoria, reported: "I have placed a Power Pole in the garden and it has increased my awareness of being one with nature."

Broadacre Towers

John McCabe of Murray Bridge, South Australia, has reported increased fertility on his farm, with sheep not needing to be drenched and the usual plagues of snails greatly reduced. He has found that the effect stops at the boundary fence. He has also had some bad effects from Towers.

Jim, a strawberry grower near Adelaide, South Australia, got a consultant in to design and locate the best spot for a Tower of Power in 1997. Since then he has been very happy with the results and has erected several more smaller Towers himself.

"Before the Tower went up my pickers would be picking 4 or 5 rows a day. After the Tower was established they could only pick 2 or 3 rows, because there was so much fruit on them!" he says. The 30 – 50% increase in fruiting could only be explained by the presence of the Tower, nothing else different had happened, nor were weather conditions any better.

Jim put some Towers in his olive tree plantation elsewhere and trees in one area that had been sickly and stunted responded immediately with flushes of new growth. Before long they had caught up with all the other olives.

Brett Siegert had 3 giant concrete Towers erected on his wheat and sheep property in the southern Eyre peninsula of South Australia. Two of them were located on upward vortices and were not doing anything perceivable to the crops. The third one seemed to have got it right. It was located over a downward vortex close to the fence line. He says that the wheat harvest is very good for around about 100 acres of the 200 acre paddock, getting thicker the closer you get to the Tower. Then at the fenceline at the back of it the effect finishes and in the next paddock the harvest has normal yields.

Another wheat farmer in Brett's region that I was told about has several Towers amongst his wheat crop. A large circular area around a Tower, where wheat grows much taller, is plain to see. At the outer edge of the Tower's energy field, in a circular band, there can be seen a step, where the wheat drops back down to its usual height.

Rain

The Americans attest to the power of Towers to make it rain more. In my own experience of building these Towers with workshop groups it has been amazing the number of times that it has rained just after completing the Tower, especially in Victoria which was in the grip of the worst drought of the century! Horsham, in the west, had very good rain a couple of days after a Tower building day, and skies over Bellingen let loose as we tried to finish a Tower there. Some people have had so much rain after Towers

170

went up that they considered pulling them. So results have been encouraging, even if a little soggy.

Victoria's drought conditions have eased somewhat, however 'normal weather' may well be a thing of the past, now that global climatic instability seems to be the norm.

Weeds

Around Jim's large Tower and at others I saw weeds growing lushly when I visited. This has happened in my own experience too, with weeds towering over the Tower and obscuring it. Searching for a Tower in my big backyard in a sea of giant ragweed I could tell I was getting close to it- when the weeds became much taller and thicker.

One was even growing out of the edge of the concrete cap, it's roots going down into the rock dust and looking very aerial-like (photo right). Elsewhere, seeing a very lush weed growing out of the brickwork of a chimney, reminds me that clay bricks are fairly paramagnetic too and good to build Towers with.

Anti-fungal effects

A Tower I helped construct in Wanneroo, Western Australia, on a 3 ha (7 ac) market garden would send "tingles down the spine" of farmer Gary de Piazzi whenever he passed by. "Cropping on the sandy coastal plain is a bit like hydroponics, because of the lack of most nutrients there", says Gary, who wanted to reduce dependance on chemical inputs, especially in the winter wet season, when moulds develop quickly in vegetables.

After the Tower went up in 1994, at a carefully selected position, and he had spread paramagnetic rock dust over cropping areas, the next winter was particularly wet, with Perth's main Mundaring dam spilling over. But Gary didn't need to use fungicide and the vegetables were more robust than ever.

Several farmers in Tasmania, where winters are cold and wet, have also enjoyed increased growth and decreased fungal problems with Towers, I have been told.

A neglected avocardo orchard near Tabulam, northern NSW was suffering from die-back due to phytothphera, a fungal infection of tree roots. Hubbertus Bobbert erected 2 Towers of Power on either end of the orchard, directly beneath the path of a 'ley line' (with one in the photo on right).

Standard PVC pipe was used, filled with paramagnetic rock dust with a copper pipe in the middle that's filled with quartz chips. About 3 m (9') tall, the Towers were crowned by a beautiful pottery cone, of curvy organic form. Just below the cone are 4 round window holes at the cardinal points. Glass jars with remedies are positioned by the copper pipe at the top and bottom of the Tower, with BD prep 501 at the bottom, for light bringing and ripening forces; while at the top the soil preps such as 500 and a phytophthera remedy were broadcasting downwards.

Paramagnetic and other rockdusts were also spread under trees, which rapidly regenerated under the new, intensified regime. When I visited there I could feel the Tower energy as we drove through the orchard, and admired its effects, in the form of lush new leaf growth. The majority of trees had been brought back from the brink of death.

Animal attraction

Animals sense the energy of Towers and love to frolic around them, or rub themselves on them (a problem with large animals like cows!) At the large concrete Tower of Dean and Lesley Gentilin's kangaroos are often seen relaxing.

After Mary and John Singer had their Tower installed at Bowning, near Canberra a lone kangaroo started to visit the Tower each sunset and would ask them for a feed. They suspect it was a pet one that had got lost during bushfires. The endearing animal put a bit of magic into their lives.

Kangaroos also enjoy the sandstone Tower at Clarrie Wooster's place and visit during the day to nibble on grass, unperturbed by the presence of humans.

At Ellen and Ray Stanyers' the fowl yard had been always a place where Ellen felt that something wasn't right, while the hens were always anxious to be let out. Ellen would think that perhaps it needed a clean up or something, but nothing seemed to help.

Realising that fencing would have stopped the energy field from their nearby Tower from coming in, they decided to erect a small Tower (half sized PVC pipe) in the yard, where dowsing suggested. As soon as the Tower went up it felt good to be in there and the hens responded by becoming very happy and contented as a consequence.

Towers can have an active healing effect, so it was not surprising that my dog Vikki was so attracted to the Tower when recovering from having 4 puppies and a hysterectomy. As soon as she could walk she would have a little daily trot only around the nearest Tower for a short time, then go straight back to the babes.

Improved sex life

When a recently divorced Canberra woman had her Tower put up in the backyard, at a location determined by dowsing, it turned out that, according to principles of feng shui, it had been positioned in the relationships corner of the magic square. The next day she met a new man who helped to take her mind away from the divorce!

Another candid owner of a Tower was very pleased to report a great improvement in the couple's sex life, after geomantic work was done and a Tower installed not far from the bedroom. He just said that sex was now very 'yang', which I assume meant much more active or boisterous perhaps, or was he too exhausted to talk about it?

It certainly made sense, considering some of the scientific studies of the effects of magnetism. Mice, it has been found, exposed to the yang energy from the south pole of magnets enjoyed increased sexual strength, vigour and fertility. Too much of that energy and they would over-indulge and die early! [4]

A central Australian Aboriginal tribe believes that sexual attraction

173

between men and women is caused by the sun goddess. [5]

Magnetite (lodestone), which is a naturally occurring magnetic rock, has also been traditionally considered sexy. It was attributed magical, sexual powers, with the Greeks believing that a man could ensure his wife's faithfulness by placing lodestone under her pillow when she slept. In Sanskrit the word for lodestone means 'kisser' and in Chinese their word for it literally translates as 'loving stone'. [6]

It is not surprising then that the forces of commercialism have cottoned on. For Horst Rechelbacher, the founder of Aveda which manufactures eco-aware cosmetics, has announced that the future lies in "vibrational substances" and that the Estee Lauder laboratories are working on putting minerals into creams to stimulate cells, and adding magnets, ground into micro-fine dust, to lotions and creams. Some will be put into lipsticks to puff up lips. [7] So lipstick and Towers may become the new sex-aids of the 21st century!

Anti-radiation

There is a sense that the paramagnetic energy field generated by Towers is able to counteract harmful electro-magnetic fields. When Towers have been installed under power lines dowsing suggests a reduction of the hazard of EMR and it generally feels less stressful there.

Likewise, in areas with geopathic stress, the energy field of the Tower seems to override these detrimental energies to some degree. More research is needed to determine the value of anti-radiation effects of Towers.

Strange Tower Effect?

Derna Godwin of Perth wrote to Geomantica in 1998 to say that it was hard to tell if her Tower had helped her garden along, as it was early days yet, but "Do I imagine it or am I feeling a bit more enthused?"

There had been one mysterious development, however. "The only event to report that might be Tower related is that a silver chain I've been wearing since about October seems to have grown! I was very happy with this chain as it made the Pau shell locket sit over a scar on my chest. It now sits 7cm (3") lower down, which makes the chain about 14cm (6") longer. I racked my brain for logical explanations but none fit. I only have one silver chain. I've accused Siggi of changing it in the night, which he denies. Why would he? - very mysterious! I wonder why I don't take the bloody thing off as it now gets caught on everything. Before it just sat there hiding my scar!"

References:

1- 'Ancient Mysteries, Modern Visions', Phil Callahan, Acres USA, 1984.
2- 'Secrets of the Soil', C. Bird and P. Tompkins, Harper and Row, USA, 1989.
3- 'Your Garden', Australia, April 1996.
4- 'Voices of the First Day – Awakening in the Aboriginal Dreamtime', Robert Lawlor, Inner Traditions, USA, 1991.
5- 'Eclipse of the Sun,' Janet Crickland, Gothic Image, UK, 1990.
6- 'The Illustrated Book of Signs and Symbols', Miranda Bruce-Mitford, Dorling Kindersley, 1996, UK.
7- 'Vogue Beauty', UK, 2000.

Cartoon by Alan Gower

4.5 Building Towers

Simple Tower designs

You can create your own Tower of Power in many ways, simply and easily. Effectiveness is determined by size, amongst other factors. For a medium sized Tower, to cover a big backyard or more, Callahan recommends to make the above ground height at least 3m (9') , to gain maximum Schumann resonance (which comes to Earth, bounces off the ground and cancels itself out for the first 3m (9'), he says).

Of course if you are making mini Towers, then Schumann resonance is not an issue. They can still transmit paramagnetism to the soil. Experiment with a cardboard tube covered with carborundum sandpaper attached with waterproof glue. The cap can be made from a circle of sandpaper, with a slit cut to the centre, that is folded into a cone shape. Mini Towers are good to place in flower pots and small gardens.

A portable Pot Tower can be good for energising a larger growing area, such as a small suburban yard. It can be simply disassembled, if it doesn't work, or if you have to move. Being made of stacked plant pots that are filled with paramagnetic rock dust, a Pot Tower will also not reach the 3m (9') mark, but can still be effective.

Whatever style of Tower you build you must never omit the broadcasting of paramagnetic rock dust within the area of Tower influence, to gain maximum soil effects. If your soil is already paramagnetic you might not need to, but it always helps.

Pipes

Many people use PVC (plastic) stormwater pipes, or old terracotta pipes, filled with basalt or other paramagnetic rock dust, as medium sized Towers. Later these can be decorated with paint or cement (such as the Tower on the right, at Lee Gray's).

176

Big fibre-cement, concrete or recycled plastic irrigation pipes can be great for large area coverage Towers.

A standard PVC pipe length of 6m (22') with a 15 cm (6") diameter is usually cut in half, to make 2 medium sized Towers. Even a quarter of a length can make an effective Tower, as Ellen found in her fowl yard. A 3m (9') pipe is sufficiently long to be sunk 60cm (2') into the ground for stability (or else cement some rocks around the base.)

I always look for second hand pipes, if I can find them, asking demolition yards etc. Not only are they a fraction of the price, but they save the use of toxic raw materials like heavy metals, which are used in PVC manufacture.

Some people fashion tailor made pipes of terracotta; a hollow log filled with rock dust would also suit. I personally don't recommend

Junitta Vallak finishes the cap of her new Tower at Maldon, Victoria.

the use of metal in Tower construction, as this could give a ferro-magnetic affect. But corrugated iron might be used as temporary form-work, into which a load of concrete, made from mostly paramagnetic rock dust, could be poured.

Some people place empty pipes (copper pipe, PVC or agricultural slotted pipe) inside the main one, to convey air or act as resonance chambers; and also put copper wires winding up inside, from the ground to the Tower top. But it is not known just how necessary they may be.

At the top of the pipe Towers that I construct a small amount of rock dust based concrete is hand worked into the shape of a conical cap, its angle either corresponding to the angle of latitude of the location, or as previously determined by dowsing. Alternatively, a mould can be made from sheet metal which can produce an infinite number of ready made caps that can sit of top of the Towers.

This does lock you in to a particular angle, so it's better if a mould can be made to be adjustable.

Masonry tower

Stone or brickwork can be used to build classic looking Round Towers. Mix paramagnetic rock dust with cement powder for the mortar. I have never bothered with the effort of making a masonry Tower, as the pipe and rock dust ones are so easy and look good when painted with acrylic paint.

Terracotta Pots

One of Callahan's students bought 7 terracotta plant pots of ascending sizes and placed them up-side-down, one on top of the other, to create a hollow Tower (like Cherese's on right).

The bottom (largest) pot rested on some bricks to enhance the upward flow of paramagnetic oxygen. The next day he noticed the ambience of the backyard garden to have subtly improved.

Cherese Haslam's
never-say-die-couch grass Tower.

Plastic Pot Tower

After Bill Nichols of Geelong, Victoria, learnt about Towers, the next day he found a dragon (energy) line in the backyard and constructed a Tower of large-to-small sized plastic pots filled with rock dust and stacked together.

He was thinking his Tower seemed a bit shakey and went out the next day to reinforce it with 3 or 4 garden stakes for security. "Would you believe it" Bill wrote in Geomantica, "just as I picked up the very first stake, the Tower fell over! Maybe it was trying to tell me something. Anyway the new Tower is now much better."

Siting Towers

When dowsing for a good location for a Tower look for a spot that has a downward pulling energy, where energy lines cross. Underground water

178

streams are good, however you mainly need to find a spot within a given area, so that there is good proximity to crops. So ask the pendulum for the best location within a given area.

Also, you need to humbly enquire through the pendulum whether it is a good idea to place the Tower where you would like it to go. Ask something like – 'Is it generally appropriate to erect a Tower in this location?'

Power Tower Energies

In the Chinese view of things, the form of the Round Tower is a symbol for the element of fire. So in feng shui terms one is putting fire into the landscape with a Tower, as you do with a pagoda, the Chinese equivalent. This has the effect of stimulating landscape energies that are overly yin, such as where there is a flat plain.

A well designed and located Tower puts out a flooding sea of yang energy that goes out in a circle around it, the area covered depending on the dimensions of the pipe.

This field flow is interrupted by any metal structures, which 'short it out'. A standard PVC pipe model may cover several acres, while a huge concrete one can affect up to around a 440ha (1000 ac) area.

Dowsing also reveals that 4 streams of more intense energy go out in the cardinal directions from the Tower within its general energy field. Our intentions can program this energy field to perform specific functions.

Sometimes I am aware of pulses of energy being emitted horizontally outwards from my Towers. There may also be a sense of weightlessness, felt when standing close with the palms pointed towards a Tower. This 'anti-gravity effect' is strongest at full moon.

Prof. Stuart Hill, international organic farming expert, dowses a Tower in Victoria.

179

The Vortex

Towers are usually located on a vortex point, which is a natural energy pattern associated with a crossing of energy lines. The vortex tends to swell in size with the erection of a Tower and with people interacting with it. Dowsing shows that the bands of the spiral widen and become more numerous.

The Earth spiral is also drawn up the Tower itself (see diagram on right), as it does on ancient standing stones and monuments, including the Irish Towers. So there's a range of interactive energetic activity going on.

Juergen Schmidt's Tower design has a magnet with the yang side pointed downwards to 'draw up the vortex below' and this magnet is connected to the apex by means of a copper wire, wound up an inner pipe in an anti-clockwise spiral. This may not be necessary, because the vortex automatically spirals up the pipe in my experience.

This phenomena happens with megalithic standing stones also, and the startling effects of dowsing the bands of energy on such stones was illustrated by the experiences of dowser/author Tom Graves, in 'Needles of Stone'.[1] Tom tells me that the seventh energy band, at the top of a standing stone, can give a dowser quite a shock when attuned to. Lower down at the fifth band dowsers can literally spin out, as they are pushed away from the stone either to the left or right. The polarity of this spin affect was found to change over every 6 days after the new and full moon times. The energy polarity was not fixed, and each dowser experienced it differently.

Looking at the photo (left) of a 'decorated stone' found at the famous

*Groundplan of Tower energies, with Earth vortex
and intense energy field streams at the cardinal points.*

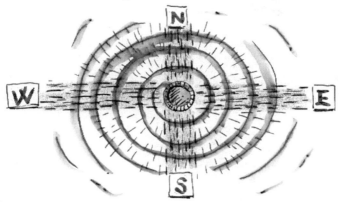

Irish passage tomb of Knowth, I can't help thinking that this carved stone is perhaps illustrating the energies of the vortex rising up a megalithic stone. Earth's energies were apparently 50% stronger some 5000 years ago, around when it was carved. Hence we can imagine the greater importance that the Earth spirit had to Neolithic peoples.

Energy door

According to energy researcher Harvey Lisle the energy door of a tree is associated with the neutral point of a magnet- located where the positively charged atmosphere meets the negatively charged Earth. He buries a jar of BD soil remedies around the roots of a tree, at the energy door, wherever there is also an Earth energy line passing through. The tree's energy field is greatly amplified by doing this. [2] However some people think of the energy door as synonymous with the fundamental ray.

The so-called energy door of a Tower seems to be something else again. It may well be at the point where the Schumann waves have stopped cancelling themself out, at about the 2.1- 2.4m (8'-9') point recommended for Tower height. And it may be an aspect of the seventh band of the vortex. Whatever it is, the energy door is found somewhere around the top of the Tower and it's exact location needs to be ascertained by dowsing.

At this energy door you can place a jar of remedies to broadcast out into the Tower's energy field. Make an actual door in the PVC, or perhaps

181

strap a jar to the outside of the pipe. Some people's Tower designs have hollow metal caps, under which the remedy jar may be placed.

You can also place a drum of water next to a Tower into which fertilising materials are added (manure, comfrey, weeds etc). Put a lid on it and allow it to ferment for a time (ask the pendulum for when it's ready.) This is said to make a really excellent liquid fertiliser, as good as 500. If the drum is placed according to dowsing, possibly in relation to the energy door/fundamental ray, the effect would probably be amplified.

Tower Rituals

Geomancer Darryl Mitchell has made the point that "if a Tower is built by a person with strong ch'i development, then its effects will be much stronger than if built by an inexperienced person, as we draw in the ch'i in time and space." [3] All the better to use the synergy of a focused group of people to build one, as in the photo, next page, of a group of happy Tower builders, in the Western Australian wheatbelt.

Ceremony and ritual are potent amplifiers of energies and intentions, and they help people to attain altered states of consciousness, which is a

prerequisite for magic happening! Getting a group of friends together to build the Tower and then consecrate it, to reinforce your intentions, is a great idea. Pick an important day in the lunar or solar calendar to do it, if possible. Full moon is perfect for a Tower ceremony, when energies are strongest.

Singing and chanting around a Tower can be aurally stunning, and meditation is also enhanced beside it. I often feel drawn to meditate by my Towers, as others are, and I then reinforce any energy field programming. Chanting seems to stimulate the Tower energies, as well as one's own.

Many times after a Tower ceremony people have been amazed to be able to actually see a dense energy field emanating from the Tower and looking somewhat like a heat haze in the atmosphere. This is due to their heightened awareness from prior working with the pendulum and the Earth and Tower energies.

Usually a lot of chatter goes on after a Tower ceremony, as participants soak up the paramagnetism, which refreshes their energy and stimulates their thinking. It can be hard to drag oneself away. If you don't feel good after building a Tower there may be something wrong with it!

Be aware that a person with strong negative thought patterns can disrupt the intentions of a Tower ceremony. So don't invite overly negative people along and make sure everyone is comfortable with what is happening, or let them drop out.

The power of our thoughts and feelings are much greater than we tend to think!

References:

1- 'Needles of Stone', Tom Graves, Turnstone, UK, 1978 (out of print).
2 - 'Agricultural Renewal', Hugh Lovel, Union Agricultural Institute, 2000.
3 - 'EMFs and Energy Towers,' Darryl Mitchell, 'Green Connections', no. 15.

4.6 Problem with Towers

Ever since Professor Callahan came to Australia in 1993 and told us about his amazing discoveries of the biological effects of paramagnetism, I've been learning about the rock dusts of Australia and have built over 50 Towers of Power across the country. There is still much research to be done, and although the Boral scientists have been trialling rock dusts, the Tower technology can still be said to be experimental.

In August 2000 I travelled to South Australia to study Towers that have been built there by various people. Imagine my disappointment when, together with English dowser Tom Graves and Dean Gentilin of Port Lincoln, I travelled around the southern Eyre Peninsula to check out several large farms with massive concrete Towers, only to find out that most of them were not working as expected. The farmers were pretty unhappy about that too.

What can be wrong?

I have found 8 areas where problems could arise with Towers, and these might account for the lack of useful effects and worse. There may well be other factors involved. Unless problems are brought out into the open and freely discussed it is difficult to make honest progress in a new field. And if people are building useless Towers then the whole field of geomancy may be brought into disrepute. (A dowser/geomancer selects their location.) So it is important to work out what is going wrong.

1) Inappropriate materials or construction?

Professor Callahan defined the Irish Round Towers as 'silicone rich semi-conductors' of cosmic energies. Some of the Towers I saw in South Australia were made with varying amounts of metal. Perhaps the substitution of silicone rich semi-conductor materials with a ferro-magnetic metal is going off track?

Also, sometimes the specifications of construction were not always followed by the farmers who built them. And perhaps the metal or concrete caps didn't have the most appropriate angle? Dowsing can be of assistance here.

2) Wrong energy point?

Callahan suggested to site Towers of Power on a downward Earth energy vortex, and/or over underground water line crossings. This traditional placement was confirmed by my own dowsing at Towers in Ireland – the water line crossings and springs all had a downward vortex at the centre associated with them.

All the Towers seen in SA were located on energy line crossings, but these were not necessarily water lines. The crossing points that had a downward vortex associated with them were in the minority. All the Towers located over the downward vortex were beneficially effective in some degree, or at the worst, just non-effective.

The quality of the energy emanating from Towers located over a positive vortex felt different, and, at worst it made some people feel sick.

Often the pendulum described an unusual star/flower patterned elliptical rotation in response to the energy field of the upward vortex – another indication of the difference in quality.

Although large, this concrete Tower was not working well enough. It was located over an upward vortex.

3) Inappropriate location?

Some of the Tower locations just seemed to be plainly inappropriate. For instance one was observed in the middle of a wetland area, adjacent to a barley field over a metal fence. The owner was happy with the crop in that paddock (although rain had been good). But approaching the Tower in the swamp, sited over an upward vortex, Tom and I felt sick in the stomach.

185

I don't think sensible dowsing protocol was applied in this case, that is - asking "May I, Should I, Can I?" before beginning the dowsing work. I usually get a 'no' if asking about the appropriateness of placing a Tower in amongst established trees, as this one was.

It would seem to be unnecessary in any case, especially if Towers are a substitute for trees, as some people assert. (According to Callahan trees and Towers both collect Schumann waves, however trees adsorb negative north monopoles from the sun, while Towers collect positive south monopoles.)

Some people contend that it is necessary to gain the consent and co-operation of the local nature spirits before Tower building and they seek devic permission beforehand.

4) Wrong motivation?

The motivations underlying the siting and design of the Power Towers could possibly be warping the effectiveness of them. Originally Towers were associated with places of great sanctity and learning in Ireland. Unethical intentions might counteract the good energy one would hope to expect from them.

5) Geological interference?

One large Tower, on a hilltop on the Eyre Peninsula with a commanding view, had a lovely, peaceful energy field around it. The owners liked to go there and meditate regularly. Positioned over the necessary downward vortex it seemed to hold much promise, yet not far out from it the energy field petered away to nothing.

What was causing this? It seemed fairly obvious when I looked at what was happening on the ground. At the point where the energy field petered out a belt of limestone started up and there was limestone over the rest of the paddock around the little hill. Being a highly diamagnetic stone, I can only conclude that the paramagnetic field of the Tower was cancelled out by the large amount of diamagnetic limestone present.

The answer to this problem is, of course, to spread paramagnetic rock dust over the paddock, and this is always recommended to maximise the efficiency of the Tower. Of course it's a lot harder to do than just build a Tower, which some people may expect to give a 'quick fix' to their crops. Unfortunately the Eyre Peninsula doesn't have gravel crushing quarries where suitable rock dust may be cheaply available.

6) Minor disturbances

Occasionally there are minor energy disturbances associated with Tower building. On some occasions some of the people who are helping with Tower construction start to feel sick, in the stomach mainly, however this has usually gone by the next day. I put it down to the massive subtle energy changes stirring people up, so it's not a big problem.

I am also aware that in some cases in my experience unhealthy plants and animals have rapidly died after the Tower was constructed. I put this down to the possibility that natural process are speeded up by the Tower. For instance a bacterial infection would no doubt be powering in the energy field of a Tower.

7) Fence line interference?

I have found that the area of Tower effectiveness is greatly reduced by metal fencing, which seems to 'interrupt the energies', as dowser T.C. Lethbridge would put it. While some disagree with this idea, it was verified by Brett Siegert, on his wheat/sheep farm on the Eyre Peninsula. Brett was getting good results, with increased wheat yields from just one of his 3 Towers, which was located over a downward vortex and very close to the fence line. Beyond the fence line in the next paddock the wheat and pastures are never as good as in the Tower paddock.

8) Ethics and ownership?

The ethics of ownership come into this question also. Should it be our intention to send an energy field over a large area, into the fields and homes of our neighbours, without their knowledge or consent? Some claim that their Towers are capable of this. But is this ethical? I think not. I find it fortunate that the typical metal fence line of our boundaries is probably going to contain the energy field we are creating with the Tower.

This question is particularly relevant when we intend to tune the energy

187

field of the Tower to only be of benefit to certain crops. The frequency might antagonise other plants. The same issue looms in the ethics of radionic broadcasts.

Someone in northern NSW once experimented with the radionic broadcasting of herbicides via their radionic device, I have been told. They broadcast the herbicide over the property, but without proper attention to boundaries. Surrounding properties were direly affected. "It resulted in considerable losses for commercial properties and much environmental damage to bush land areas" my informant, radionic researcher Gil Robertson of Port Lincoln, told me.

I have heard of the odd Tower making the crop it was supposed to be enhancing sicken. So the idea of owning the energies we are responsible for and keeping them neatly within our boundaries is very important.

Conclusion

There is no point in gung ho enthusiasm with this experimental technology, and we must beware of premature commercial exploitation. Not enough really good research has been done on Towers to be able to guarantee their effectiveness.

I am, however, convinced of the value of further experimentation with Towers and think that scientifically styled research is long overdue in this field. We don't, for instance, know how critical location, design etc are for success. Properly controlled field trials need to be set up, so that farmers can embrace the technology with confidence in the future.

I have seen many effects gained from the Towers, some wonderful, some mediocre, and some non-effects. I am very keen to learn more of any 'negative'/ detrimental effects that people have experienced, because this is how we learn to get it right.

References:

Geomantica no 10.   *Cartoon by Alan Gower*

PART FIVE: FARMERS of the FUTURE

5.1 Amazing Olives

Biodynamic farmer Pia Lindgrew lives in the Hunter Valley of NSW, near Pokolbin, a renowned wine growing district. Her farm was purchased some 3 years ago with husband Greg, and currently has 6000 young olive trees, with plans for another 6000. To her knowledge it's the largest privately owned biodynamic olive grove in NSW. The farm is a shining example of enhanced biodynamics and Pia is active in spreading the word about their success.

The bare pastures of Pia's farm had been used for cattle grazing for many years before, which was good because this involved no toxic chemical usage. Soil testing was their first undertaking and from day one they started to spray the biodynamic 500, always applying it at the time of the descending moon. To build up the soil before the olives went in, the ground was cross deep ripped and fowl manure, dolomite and some local basalt rock dust, at 12 tonnes to the hectare (6 tons to the acre), were all incorporated into the soil. Several legume and other cover crops were continuously grown and turned in before maturing, to enhance organic matter and soil nutrient levels.

While a commercial crop such as olives may sound like a standard monoculture, the intensive soil building practises of biodynamic farming create a polycultural component that is not so obvious to the unknowing eye. So the single crop is supported by a soil polyculture.

After turning in the cover crop in spring 1999, they then had to set up the paddocks, marking out the trees' planting positions at 5 m by 8 m (17' - 27') intervals. When finally everything was ready they were able to plant the trees in early October 1999. The trees were delivered when they were about 50cm (knee high) soft cuttings and the first thing was to water them in their pots with liquid 500. Into the planting holes organic blood and bone was added and more liquid 500 was used to water in the

189

newly planted trees.

"We were not meant to do anything to the trees for one year after that, apart from caring for the soil and cover crops," Pia said, "but it wasn't long before we started freaking out, because by Christmas the trees had just about doubled in height and there were thick side shoots on them, which is just about unheard of in the olive growing world - it usually takes about a year! Because we are a commercial size operation and were not meant to do any tree work for a year it was a bit disconcerting, because we didn't have any employees lined up to help out. So at Christmas time we went out and started to prune the side shoots off. If we didn't they would eventually interfere with mechanical harvesting, which requires 1.2m (4') clearance under the trees. We talked to a lot of experts who said we had to do this."

"Olives Australia, the biggest olive growers in Australia, who ship out 25,000 trees every week, are now doing research on our property because they are so amazed at the growth their trees have attained here. According to the soil test our soil isn't bad, but it's not wonderful either. But Olives Australia do understand that rock dust is an important soil additive, and that with it the olives grow much better (although they don't know about the beneficial paramagnetic energy of the rock dust). So they already recommend that their trees are planted in with some rock dust".

"But we had to complain to Olives Australia because when they arrived there is a bamboo stake tied on to each tree with bits of tape, and when they had the explosive growth the tape started to strangle the base of each tree! And so for all the 6000 trees we had to cut off each piece of tape. When we asked them about it they said 'no way- the tape should break down in a year's time, and trees never outgrow it'. Well we showed them photos of our tree's growth and they were flabbergasted! They are now doing some experimentation on the property, with the rock dust and the 500, to see for themselves what happens. It will be interesting to see what will come out of that."

"People are always stopping on the road and coming to ask us, 'weren't those trees planted just a year ago, what have you done to get that growth?' so there has been much interest from the locals" Pia enthused. "Because we do it organically and are very involved with the Hunter Valley Olive Association (the largest regional olive group in Australia), word got around and soon we were approached by Boral, the big construction company, who heard about what was happening here. They heard that we were using the rock dust, and they have a rock dust product called Nu-Soil, which we have used as well. Because we've had fantastic results they asked if they could do some research here. So now Boral have started doing a ten year trial here, with their agronomists, and we have test plots where we don't use any rock dust or 500 for microbes, and a plot where we do. Time will tell, because we believe that we will get a better oil from using these soil amendments, and Boral will be testing that oil."

Paramagnetism

Boral's geologist Tony Zdrilic, who works on the Nu-Soil research, has the wholistic approach that biodynamic farmers like Pia also embrace. He told me that he believes the rock dust is very valuable, but not in isolation. With added microorganisms, plus organic matter to feed them, the biological digestive processes in the living soil are greatly enhanced, and are complemented by the minerals and energy provided by the selected paramagnetic rock dusts. The BD 500 used by Pia is a powerful microbial stimulant and Boral is producing its own microbial soil additive. Tony also believes that Towers of Power can assist the activity of soil life and enhance the paramagnetic energy imparted by the rock dusts. I asked Pia if the Tower of Power I had built near her house just over a year before had had any perceivable effects.

"Our Tower is away from the olives here, but we do intend to build one up in the olive grove because we believe that we'll have very good effects from this. When we put the Tower up I personally felt sick and nauseous for a short while after. I'm a very sensitive person and for me this was a positive thing, because I know when I feel like this that some energy is being moved, and so, it may sound strange, but I quite

welcome that feeling. So I knew that the Tower was very powerful."

"At the time we had just had 6 months with hardly any rain here and it was very, very dry. I think it was about a week after that it started to rain and it kept on raining and raining and it got to the point that we couldn't get tractors out or anything. It was just odd, an odd time of year to rain so much, and Greg was joking that we should take the Tower down. Whether it was a coincidence or whether the Towers actually do help it to rain, well, I really do not know…"

"Good people keep being attracted to this place, since the Tower went up" Pia continued "So there's good energy always coming in."

I suppose like attracts like, because I could feel the good energy present there as soon as I drove onto the property, and observed a mob of kangaroos relaxing happily at twilight.

Farmworker Ernie has been enjoying enhanced health since coming to live on the farm. For years he has suffered debilitating chronic back pain, from an accident. Since working in the rock dusted fields he has been improving and now walks for miles every day, having filled the soles of his shoes with rock dust! He sleeps better than he ever has there, since placing a bag of rock dust under his bed.

Pia has also experimented with other uses for rock dust. She did some trials with sprouting organic wheat and the most impressive sprouts, that were bursting out of their box, had had rock dust and 500 added to them.

Pia's neighbour makes their own 500 on their biodynamic farm. They use sloppy green cow manure, with some rock dust, clay and a little 500 added, then stuff the mixture into cow horns and bury them over winter. For the last mix they had run out of 500 towards the end, but used the mixture without it for the last few horns. When the horns were dug up a season later all the mix had transformed into 500 - it was black, crumbly and smelt wonderful. But in the horns that had missed out on their 500, the mixture was still as green and sloppy as when it had went in.

5.2 Organic Dairying

Visiting Ron and Bev Smith's 86ha (200 ac) organic dairy farm in Fish Creek, South Gippsland is like arriving at a lush oasis. All around, the neighbours' paddocks were baking in the sun after 18 months of drought and they had been trucking in water for several months. At the Smith's farm the huge keyline dams may only have been 20% full, but they still provided plenty of water for irrigation.

In 1980 the family had been forced to stop using chemical fertilizers because of the asthmatic reactions Ron experienced whenever he applied them. Thus they began to convert to organic methods, ceasing to use synthetic inputs altogether. By 1989 they had gained full organic certification with N.A.S.A.A.

Marketing was quite a challenge, with Sandhurst Farms eventually taking them on in 1992 to retail Australia's first organic milk. The milk is now sold in cartons in many Victorian supermarkets, as well as further afield. Ron and Bev are justifiably proud of their pioneering achievements.

When they first leased the farm in 1978 the land was in a very poor, degraded state. However they persevered and took up an option to buy in 1980. Soil tests at that time revealed a highly acid soil, with a pH of 3.9 and a topsoil depth of only 50mm (2"). They began on a steep learning curve, attending seminar and field days to increase knowledge of soil health. Nowadays the topsoil goes down to 200mm (8"), has a good structure and an optimum pH of 6 to 6.5.

Keyline planning

In order to work from a sound basis they had a whole farm plan drawn up in 1980 and built a 20 megalitre (3.6 million gal) dam for stock and domestic water, to hold some of the annual 110mm (44") of mainly winter rain. Ken Yeomans was brought in to develop a keyline design.

The concept of keyline irrigation is to place dams at the highest appro-priate position in a valley - the 'keypoint'- and to run contour channels out from the base of the dam wall. Water is flood irrigated thence from the dam along the channels, with a system of flags used to control water flow. Ripping is done along contours to increase surface water infiltration and prevent erosion.

In 1983 a huge 130 megalitre (30 million gal) dam was built for keyline irrigation. It covers 3.5 ha (8 ac) when full and has a 1 km (.8 mile) perimeter. Two channels start at the dam wall (seen above), where a 40 cm (16") lock tap delivers water from pipe installed under the dam wall.

One channel runs east at a slight slope of 1:500 for 600 m (600 yds), the other runs west at 1:2000 for 2.1 km (1.4 mile). The flood irrigation is always done on the day after either the full or new moon, with 4 ha (10 ac) irrigated each hour - that's 30,000lt (6,600 gal) a minute!

Along the channels and between paddocks 12,000 trees have been planted in 4km (2.5 miles) of shelterbelts that undulate along the contours of the land. Scraggly remnant bush in some areas was fenced in 1978 and is now thick and healthy. Frogs and birds have returned in great numbers. Thirty different frog calls have been identified after rain!

"I hate seeing straight lines" says Ron, looking at shelterbelts that were initially planting across the contour. "Because the land slopes down to the south-east, where the prevailing winds originate from, it's really best to run the shelterbelt along the contour and thus break the wind."

Soil Magic

To restore fertility to the soil the Smiths are very diligent in balancing soil nutrients. The once exhausted, compacted soil is now loose, with abundant soil life and about 50 worms to the shovelfull. Pasture is thick, with deep rooted swards of clover, grass and chicory all having sturdy, solid stems. Plants have high mineral sugar content- which deters pests from attacking (as shown by Brix levels). Fertilizers only cost them about $AUD12,000 each year, as compared to $AUD35-45,000 for a conventionally run dairy farm of the same size.

They use the Albrecht system of soil balancing, with soil testing done at Brookside Laboratories in the USA. This test establishes the cation exchange capacity of soil, from which a prescription mix of mineral fertilisers is worked out. Soil pH levels are adjusted by improving nutrient balance, as opposed to the simplistic method of liming. Animals that graze on the balanced pastures enjoy good health. The Smiths rarely need to call in the vet, Whereas an equivalent non-organic farm might spend $AUD5-10,000 on a year's vet bills. Ron only has to assist a cow with calving about once each year .

If pastures start to look stressed Ron applies a tonic in the form of liquid Sea Minerals- a concentrated dose of sea water with reduced sodium levels. "This only works if phosphate and calcium levels are in order" says Bev.

Weeds are also not a great problem, but if necessary a gas flame thrower or slashing is used for control.

Paramagnetism

Perhaps the single most important soil fertilizer used by the Smiths is rock dust from the quarry at Mt Schank, near South Australia's Mt Gambier. It delivers a wide range of minerals and trace elements, but it is the excellant paramagnetic qualities that set it above others.

Ron spreads 1.5 tonnes to the hectare (1/2 ton to the acre) every five years or so and is very enthusiastic about the results. "The pasture rarely wilts" he says, "and that's proof that the paramagnetism imparted into the soil from the rock dust has reduced evaporation rates."

Water problems

Lack of water was an early problem, solved by building the massive storage dams. Later the dams became infested in deadly blue-green algae, caused by effluent run-off from a next door piggery. When EPA designated effluent ponds were installed the algae was reduced, but the problem kept returning.

The Smiths now achieve control with a biennial programme - placing bales of organic barley straw around the edge where surface water runoff seeps in. This introduces healthy bacteria which combat the algae. The large dam gets 30 bales - half in spring and half in late autumn. Stately black swans gliding over the water seemed to approve.

Energised water

More recently the Smiths have employed a 'Living Water Unit' for all the household and trough

water. Designed by Austrian Johann Grander, the water energiser is said to restore water's natural energies to something like that of natural spring water.

Incorporating inspiration from the work of Schauberger, Schwenk, Tesla and Hahnemann, Grander's system involves a permanent liquid magnetic field and the principle of implosion. It requires no electricity, filters or chemicals to operate. A beneficial energy field is imparted to the water that is easily perceived by dowsing over the polypipe. Kirlian photograghy reveals a highly organised pattern to this water. Improved health and farm production have resulted from its use.

"Given a choice the cows will only drink energised water and they love it!" says Ron, whose 11 children enjoy it too - and all abound with health and vitality. The family also mix a little rock dust into their drinking water for added minerals and energies.

With the energised water used to wash out dairy effluent, bacteria and pollution is reduced. The lack of manure odour was obvious. With a little hydrogen peroxide (at 50% strength) added for washing milking equipment, there is only a minimal need for detergents. Ron and others are now trying to educate politicians on the need for this technology for the general community.

Keeping cows healthy

Keeping the 150 odd cows healthy and happy is easy, considering the high quality water and pasture they consume. Feed is supplemented by sweet smelling bales of biodynamic lucerne and hay shipped all the way from Narrandera in NSW.

The Smiths use several other health supplements at different times. They are great exponents of such old fashioned remedies as apple cider vinegar, not the distilled kind, but the original fermented vinegar that retains the 'mother' plant. They get through 1000 litres (220 gal) each year! The family alone consumes 25lt (5 gal) of this. Given to cows, especially when calving, the vinegar promotes suppleness and speeds up calving considerably. Homeopathic liquid Arnica is also given when calving. If cows look poorly they are given either a little vinegar or hydrogen peroxide in water.

Cows are never vaccinated and are not worried by worms. However Ron did pass on a natural drench recipe which is ocasionally used. It is enough for one cow, and is given over 4 consecutive days:

<u>Cow 'Pick Me Up' / Drench</u>
* 1 cup dolomite
* 1 cup vinegar
* 1 cup molasses
* 1 cup water, stirred into solution.
Add to this -
* a quarter cup Maxicrop
* a quarter cup granulated yeast
* plus some salt if you wish.
For milk fever you can add one tablespoon of mono sodium phosphate.

Also worth passing on is <u>Ron's stock lick recipe</u>.
* one part each of dolomite, vinegar and molasses,
* plus a quarter part each of volcanic rock dust and salt
* plus a tenth part of kelp powder.
* To this you can also add a few pinches of elemental sulphur.

197

Ron is very much 'in tune' with his herd and can sense any distress, even when out in town. He naturally senses the need for pasture tonics also.

"There's a weather change coming, it'll probably rain Friday" Ron announced when a flock of black cockatoos arrived on Tuesday. By Thursday night it was raining. In a time when the climate is so unpredictable, it is obviously very handy to understand nature's cues.

The milk

The Smith's 100 mostly Fresian milking cows produce 500,000 litres (110,000 gal) of organic milk each year. The average number of lactations is 8 and some milkers are 10 to 12 years old- this is much higher and older than non-organic herds. The milk has very high nutritive levels. Chromaphotography reveals that it has 10 times the levels of enzymes and amino acids.

It is sold unhomogenised, for health reasons. "When you homogenise milk" Bev explained "the enzyme Xanthine oxidase is broken down into very fine particles that the body can't excrete. When it's absorbed into the bloodstream it attacks the heart and clogs arteries."

The lifestyle

Ron and Bev enjoy the very demanding and challenging lifestyle of organic dairying, with seemingly boundless energy and enthusiasm. They are raising a large family of very fit, healthy and intelligent children in an atmosphere of love and harmony.

Knowing that their produce is contributing to other people's health gives them a great peace of mind and they happily share their knowledge. Ron can often be heard speaking at conferences or farm field days, spreading the word on organics. There is a constant interaction with other organic farmers, with daily phone calls, letters and magazines from around Australia and the world.

The Smith family's farm, and their lives, are definately inspirational.

5.3 *Wheat in the Mallee*

The Mallee country in the far north west corner of Victoria, is semi-arid, flat, scrubby country that stretches across into South Australia and is bound to the north by the irrigated richness of the Murray River lands. To the south, national parks of desert wilderness have their own native richness, with glorious wildflowers in spring.

The Mallee gum, which characterises these parts, has an extremely tough lignotuber which allows the small tree to cope with drought and resprout after fires that are sparked by the lightning of dry summer storms.

When the wheat farmers moved into these marginal lands they struggled to rip out the Mallee gums as fast as possible. The famous Mallee roots were shipped to Melbourne for firewood and to England to make pipes from. With the loss of much of the tree cover the area's annual rainfall has declined by about one third.

In these parts it is not uncommon to drive through huge swirling clouds of topsoil that blow up after the hint of rain gets farmers out ploughing. Instead of bringing rain, the winds snatch up the topsoil and send it east, to dump it in the Tasman sea or on New Zealand (- no wonder that country is so lush!) I remember being in Melbourne in 1983 when severe dust storms blackened the daytime sky as if night had fallen.

The duststorms used to be far worse, going for days on end - filling houses and covering fences and roads. Farmers have been trying to modify their destructive European ways, since the severe drought of 1902, when fallowing and trash retention were introduced to conserve soil moisture and reduce the dust hazard.

The situation is not getting better, quite the opposite. With farmers not getting much for wool, many are expanding their wheat cropping to make up for the shortfall. (Some farmers are calling sheep 'land lice' these days.) When the last traces of topsoil have blown, where will the bread on our tables come from? The rape of somewhere else?

Permaculture outpost

In the heart of this so-called Sunset Country, on the Mallee Highway to Adelaide, lies the sleepy little town of Murrayville - a mistaken identity, as it is far from the Murray River. Dominated by huge wheat silos, like others nearby, this town of some 310 souls is surprisingly green. Many ancient Mallee gums have been retained throughout and actively conserved by locals. Rare native plants have survived here and many birds, such as the Rainbow Bee-eater, abound.

An abundant supply of fresh bore water makes gardening relatively easy. The loosely defined Mediterranean climate can, however, get very hot for long spells - up to 48°C (120°F). Annual rainfall is only 250 - 300mm (10 - 12"). Up to 30 frosts are experienced each winter.

Like a small oasis, Murrayville is nestled amongst huge tracts of wheat and cereal croplands. What the casual visitor may not realise is that there are many thousands of acres of organically produced crops in the area. If you were to fly over, you would be pleasantly surprised to see extensive shelter plantings of endemic species. Even 4 ha (20 ac) plus spirals of saltbush here and there.

When I visited, a local was amazed to report seeing, from a light plane above, the giant word LOVE marked out in freshly ploughed ground below him.

The 'pioneer species' responsible for initiating such Earth-centred activities, is one Kymbo Kingdon, a member of one of Murrayville's multi-generational farming families. With a 6 ha (30 ac) property on the edge of town that he and wife Kylie manage, a young family, a seed collection and tree

200

planting business and now sole responsibility for his parent's 440 ha (1000 ac) wheat and sheep farm, Kymbo is kept very busy.

A traditionally raised farmer's son, Kymbo has been developing permacultural alternatives for 10 years now and his results have been outstanding. Running the family farm for the last 8 years under an organic regime has proved very successful, with consistent increases in profit margins and protein levels. Another local farmer who grows 100% organically has retrofitted his soils so remarkably that he's considering changing from cereals to legumes, I was told.

Kymbo focusses on remineralizing his soil using a product which is a mixture of rock dusts, and also adds a micro-organism activator. A few wheat farmers in the area have successfully installed Towers of Power and are using special basalt rock dust from Mt Gambier, to the south, as their only soil additive.

The old days

In 1935 Kym's granddad Laurie bought the family farm where his mother was later born."Back then" he told me, "we used to get 16" of rain a year. Now it's only 12" to 13"." He reminisced about the severe droughts of the 30's and 40's and the straw bale house someone built 40 years ago in Pinnaroo (22km away). Before the advent of the tractor, Laurie used to manage 18 draught horses to take the wheat to market, and life revolved around them. He also kept greyhounds, a few pigs and thousands of broiler fowl, to take advantage of the abundant wheat.

When stubbble burning was outlawed, sheep were used to knock down the stubble. Fields were rested for 2 years out of 3. But with the rise of chemical farming, the rotation was reduced to a 2 year cycle. Now Kymbo has restored it back to 3 years.

For over 5 years Kymbo has been active in the Landcare movement. Now only the flat farm areas carry wheat and any higher ground is cloaked in the perennial shrubs Old Man and Curly Leaved Saltbush - sheep fodder favourites. Once the lambs were very vulnerable to attack from crows and foxes. Kymbo brought in just one alpaca to live with the flock and since then they've had no losses to predators.

Institute vision

The sceptics and traditionalists often say that the transition to organics just can't be done, or it's too difficult. But here are showpieces of sustainable broadacre farming and a Drylands Permaculture Institute in the making. Annual Permaculture Design Courses have been taught here by Kymbo (when he has the time!).

"Murrayville is a peaceful, friendly place," I was told. "There are plenty of cheap homes and cottage industry opportunities. The Neighbourhood House is superbly equipped and offers many courses. A recent 'Women in Permaculture' course was well attended. A Community Co-op is in process of establishment and The Olde Bakery will be re-opened as a bakery/ cafe/ crafts/ esoterica retail centre and gathering place."

Even Murrayville's school is a centre for permaculture, the campus being surrounded by beautiful organic gardens, with some farm animals too. Deputy principal Ian Thomson is a keen advocate, responsible for permaculture running rampant in the secondary college grounds.

Kymbo has identified an exciting range of industry opportunities for the region, in his quest to make Murrayville a centre for permaculture innovation and application. Organic flour milling, herb production (- Australia imports around 90% of its requirements!), eucalpytus and olive oil production, saltbush extraction (- it has twice the mineral content of seaweed!) and eco-tourism are all feasible.

In the meantime all are welcome to visit, stay awhile, WWOOF, or come to live and help share in the vision. "We need workers, investors, volunteers and permaculture minded people with enthusiasm and lots of energy," says Kymbo. His grand vision is well and truly on its way.

To contact the Drylands Permaculture Institute -
phone Kymbo and Kylie Kingdon 03 5095 2199

5.4 CERES - in the city

CERES is an unique, award winning 4 hectare Environment Park which is the most visited environmental education centre in Australia. In early 2000 it took out a national prize in the National Community Link Awards, sponsored by the National Australia Bank. The prize winning project was their 'Return of the Sacred Kingfisher Festival'. This event really characterises the CERES approach - helping reinforce the spirit of place and bring people closer to nature and balance with the land.

With Australia leading the world in greenhouse gas emissions, CERES has been operating a global warming program for some 9 years, with a Greenhouse Trail and Sustainable Energy House for people to probe the impact of their lifestyle choices. A renewable Energy Park is abuzz with appropriate energy systems.

The Centre is located on waste land - an ex-rubbish dump and before that a bluestone quarry, now revegetated, with giant powerlines running through the middle of it. Many of the 300 volunteers that help out in the gardens, demonstration sites and administration have had to endure high

levels of electro-magnetic stress from the power line radiation. Signage here and there alerts visitors to these radiation levels, which are expressed in milligaus. Levels of prolonged exposure above 2-3 mG are hazardous and can cause cancer and reduce immunity levels.

In late 1999 CERES staffer Ric Corinaldi asked me if I could put in a Tower of Power in the Honey Lane organic gardens where he works, directly under the power lines. Plants were growing lushly there, what with the stimulating effects of paramagnetic basalt soil and power line radiation.

Ric had been warned by his kinesiologist that as long as he was fit and well his body would be able to cope with the radiation, but not to go there if he was rundown. Hopefully the Tower would have an effect of reducing the radiation load. After it was constructed there was an immediate shift in the atmospheric feel of the site. No change in the high CellSensor (milligaus) reading, yet there was a sense of improvement. A year later, and Ric reports that the gardens have prospered, and that staff and the numerous volunteers are very happy there.

Fridays is volunteers day in the Honey Lane Garden and from between 10 am and 4 pm the day is spent planting, harvesting and implementing soil improvement techniques. Fresh organic fruit and vegetables grown there are sold at the thriving CERES Organic Market, held every Saturday morning from 9 am, at the CERES stables.

I recommend a visit to CERES to gain practical insights, enjoy the city farm atmosphere, the lush community gardens... and do a little dowsing perhaps, to check out the energy in the gardens under the power lines and around the Tower. It's open to the public to wander around every day of the week and the bush tucker nursery and cafe are also well worth checking out.

Harnessing the sun - the way of the future-
a solar cooker at CERES in Melbourne,
where the public can view sustainable
gardens and technologies, and even
a Tower of Power!

CERES
Environmental Park,
8 - 10 Lee St, East
Brunswick, Vic. 3057.
Ph 03 9387 2609.

Website:
www.ceres.org.au

Glossary:

Agnihotra – an Indian system of purification, healing and vitalisation for people, places, plants and animals which is based on the regular practice of Homa (fire) ceremonies.

Alchemy – processes of magical transmutation and the search for an elixir of life.

Biodynamic – a system of eco-agriculture originally promulgated by Rudolph Steiner. There are over one million hectares of biodynamic farmlands in Australia.

Blind spring – also known as a water dome or source, this is where underground water rises up and then spreads out along fissures, in a pattern like an octopus or a wheel, as determined by dowsing.

Brix – this is a measure of the sugar levels in plants, with high levels bestowing improved flavour, reduced predation by insects and increased frost resistance.

Carborundum – Prof. Callahan made mini Towers of Power with sandpaper of artificial carborundum, which is paramagnetic. In the shops it may be sold as garnet paper.

Ch'i - Earthly and atmospheric energies are collectively referred to as ch'i by the Chinese. In other cultures prana, od or orgone may be referring to the same thing.

Cosmic pipe – is a radionic device designed to broadcast the energies of various crop and soil remedies to farmland.

Diamagnetic – substances which are weakly repulsed by a magnet are diamagnetic. The presence of diamagnetic and paramagnetic substances in soil ensures a dynamic energetic interplay, which provides good conditions for plant growth. The great majority of plants are diamagnetic.

Dolmen – burial mound chambers incorporating massive boulders and timbers, covered over with earth in rectangular, oval or trapezoid shapes. Built from about 10,000 years ago along Europe's western seaboard.

Dowsing – The ability to tap into intuitive sources of knowing as well as perceive electro-magnetic energies, known to science as the bio-physical or bio-resonance method.

Earth-spirited permaculture – a combination of sustainable, productive landscape design with geomantic understandings of the spirit of place.

ELF – extremely low frequency energies ranging from 1Hz (cycle per second) to 10,000Hz.

Feng shui – pronounced 'foong shway' or foong soy', this is the Chinese art of geomancy, of harmonious form and placement, in relation to Earth and planetary energies.

Geomancy – the subtle forces in the landscape, the spirit of place. In modern practice it considers the effects of all environmental energies, whether natural or man-made, on our health and wellbeing.

Geomantica – subjects related to geomancy, from folk customs to monuments and artefacts.

Geopathic - zones of unhealthy Earth energies, usually flowing in streams.

Homodynamics – Steven Guth coined this term to describe the energetic interactions between Thai Buddhist monks, the community and the crops in a Thai village.

Humus - a major component of good topsoil, humus is the colloidal complex of composting organic materials where the soil's greatest fertility and moisture retention is found.

Magnetic susceptibility – the ability of a substance to receive, hold and transmit magnetic fields from the Earth and cosmos.

Microbial inoculants – cultured concentrations of particular microbes for certain purposes, eg inoculant mixed with seeds of legume plants ensures the presence of symbiotic mycorrhizal bacteria, which assist the nitrogen-fixing ability of the plant and live in plant roots. The biodynamic preps, such as 500, also act as a microbial innoculants for soil in some degree, as does compost.

Natural resonance – When 2 objects are in harmony, having the same frequencies or a harmonic of those frequencies, they vibrate in unison (resonate), leading to an increase in energy levels. Natural resonance refers to the use of natural substances used to achieve this resonance effect.

Orgone – a term for environmental energies coined by American researcher Wilhelm Reich, who invented orgone accumulators which cured cancer. He was gaoled for his trouble and died a broken man.

Paganism - pagan simply refers to the people 'of the land' and their nature based spirituality, which honours the spirits of place and the forces of Heaven and Earth.

Paramagnetism – the weak attraction to a magnet by a non-ferro-magnetic substance, i.e. it is not dependent on the presence of iron, nickel or cobalt. Paramagnetism imparts to soil magnetic susceptibility, which is life enhancing, and therefore fertility inducing.

Permaculture – a design system for productive, sustainable environments that has been modelled on nature.

Prana – this is the general Indian term for environmental and personal energies, e.g. pranayama is the yoga of breathing and when we take air deeply into our lungs we are increasing our energy levels, because oxygen is highly paramagnetic.

Radiesthesia – an old fashioned term for dowsing, allying it to radio reception. Agricultural coils are sometimes called radiesthetic coils.

Radionics – a form of advanced dowsing practice, this is a systematic method of remotely testing degrees of health/harmony and disease, via a 'witness', and then 'broadcasting' energies which can neutralise disease conditions, or impart improved fertility, to people, livestock, soil and crops.

Resonance method – or bio-resonance method, is a modern scientific term for dowsing.

Sirius mystery – the Sirius star system is very distant and 2 out of the 3 major stars in it are not visible to the eye, yet the Dogon tribe of west Africa have intimate knowledge of them. Widespread myths and legends of amphibious gods point to the possibility of some of our cultural origins deriving from there in the distant past.

Schumann waves – ELF radio waves, generated by lightning, in the 8, 14, 21, 27 and 33Hz range.

Scoria – molten volcanic rock, which has rapidly cooled – i.e. lava rock.

Terrestial zodiac – a combination of man-made plus natural features of the landscape, usually in a large circular form, which suggests a map of the constellations above, usually in the form of astrological figures, that are delineated by roads, rivers, hills, boundaries etc. The pattern of incidence of Round Towers in Ireland suggests a star map of the northern sky at winter solstice, says Prof. Callahan.

'Tesla cylinder' - cylindrically shaped object, manufactured under Dr Felsenreich's directions, comprising selected rock dusts, humic materials (from grape remains), various homeopathic preparations and other materials and used by the Natural Resonance Study groups. It activates and amplifies natural energies created by the 'Resonating Compost Heap' and helps minimise noxious effects of harmful radiations.

Witness – when testing for something by dowsing or radionic means, a photo of the subject person, animal or place, or a small piece of a substance which is sought, provides the 'witness', or the sample, by which one is able to attune/resonate with the subject.

Yang - yang forces are stimulating, active and expansive. In electro-magnetic terms they are energetically 'positive', although this does not necessarily translate as 'good'. Paramagnetism is a yang force.

Yin – the opposite complementary energy to yang, yin forces are more subtle and contractive, and energetically called 'negative', although his does not necessarily mean 'bad' energy. Diamagnetism is a yin force.

About the book and author

This book evolved from articles in quarterly magazines – 'Dowsing News', 'Earth Spirit Quarterly' and 'Geomantica' – produced by Alanna Moore from 1983 till the present. The author has gained many insights from her own research, travels, teaching and writing, and meeting with eco-farmers and geomancers around Australia.

Alanna discovered dowsing in London in 1980 and helped to found the NSW Dowsing Society in 1984. Since then she has trained many thousands of people in the art of dowsing and geomancy. In the mid '80's she began studying bush regeneration, permaculture and organic growing. Since 1991 she has been writing articles for several permaculture and rural magazines, and now produces her own books, magazine and videos, as well as running a correspondence course. Her book 'Backyard Poultry – Naturally, has been a best-seller.

Alanna has worked as an environmental campaigner for several organisations, including Greenpeace (Sydney), plus the Aboriginal land rights support movement. She is a passionate believer in 'stone age' solutions to global environmental mismanagement, and urges people to focus on creating a society and an agriculture that are firmly based on principles of bio-diversity and sustainability.

Dowsing Group Contacts -

Dowsers' Club of South Australia- PO Box 2427 Kent Town, SA 5071.

Dowsers' Society of NSW - PO Box R1369 Royal Exchange, NSW 1225.

Dowsing Society of Victoria - PO Box 4278, Ringwood, Vic 3134.

American Society of Dowsers - PO Box 24 Danville, Vermont, 05828-0024, USA.

British Society of Dowsers- c/o Sycamore Cottage, Tamley Lane, Hastingleigh, Ashford, Kent, TN25 UK.

New Zealand Society of Dowsers - POBox 41-095, St Lukes Square, Mt Albert, Aukland 3, NZ.

Hands-on training with Alanna Moore

Are you sleeping in a safe place? Find out when author and professional geomancer Alanna Moore comes to a town near you to run training sessions on attuning to environmental energies.

Geomancy is the study of Earth's subtle energies and Alanna specialises in geomancy and dowsing training- helping people to develop their intuitive faculties and energy awareness.

Participants are shown how to connect with the spirit of the land, understand its impact on their health and happiness and also how to enhance soil energy.

Geomancy helps us to appreciate the subtle qualities of landscape from a more Aboriginal perspective.

Modern geomancy also considers feng shui (Chinese geomancy) and the impact of the high-tech environment on peoples' health- from 'sick building syndrome' to the electro-magnetic radiation from computers and other common appliances.

Dowsing (also known as water divining) is an important tool used by geomancers and techniques of pendulum dowsing will be imparted in the morning workshop.

Alanna Moore offers:

A) *One and a half hour evening slideshow talks:*
'Geomancy, Paramagnetism & Towers of Power'

B) *3 hour practical training sessions*
(held on weekend mornings & afternoons)

1) 'Earth Dowsing'
Learn pendulum and map dowsing
Understand geomancy & Earth energies
Apply dowsing to soil testing etc.

2) 'Paramagnetic Gardening'
How paramagnetism induces soil fertility.
How to select rock dusts.
How Towers of Power can boost growth.
Build a simple Tower of Power!

Fee for each training sessions - $30, concession $20, $45 for couples.
Books, magazines, videos and pendulums will be on sale.

C) *Geomancy/dowsing consultancy*
Have your home or property checked out energetically, fee- $50 per hour.
Average consultancy 1-2 hours (plus travel time @ $18 hour).

To find out about attending, or hosting a workshop at your place,
(hosts attend for free and get a Tower built) or about dowsing surveys:

Contact Alanna Moore
email: info@geomantica.com
Or write to
Geomantica
PO Box 929
Castlemaine
Vic. 3450
Australia.

New books from Python Press:

Earthspirit Australia by Alanna Moore

Geomancy is the art of addressing the subtle energies of the natural environment. It is derived from the perceptions of ancient peoples the world over, and in the 21st century, it incorporates insights into the potential dangers of the highly technological environment also. Geomancers interpret the spirit of place and advise on how to avoid geopathic and electro-stress zones, and have energetically healthy homes and workspaces.

Fig Tree Spirit, from the story of the Children of the Trees organisation (Sydney), photo Chris Farmer.

While the Chinese art of feng shui geomancy is now fairly well known and often practised in Australia, we tend to forget that there is an indigenous geomancy which evolved with Aboriginal culture over tens of thousands of years. A complex network of sacred sites, dreaming tracks and songlines covers the continent. In many parts of the country the memory of these geomantic structures has been wiped out. But still the energies, nature spirits and Earth memories may remain. Build your home over a desecrated site and you may well be plagued with problems of all kinds. Understand the problem - and a solution may be divined.

Mining, quarrying and other earthworks can unhinge the harmony of a whole district by their energetic effects. So in order to truly tread lightly upon the Earth we must find ways to respect the spirit of place and live and work more in harmony with it, for the wellbeing of all.

Earthspirit Australia looks at these issues and more. It describes the various forms of the Earth spirit, from noxious rays to benign dragon spirals and 'Earth acupuncture' points. It profiles geomancers and their work, both here and overseas. There are tips on how to deal with geopathic stress, desecrated Aboriginal sites and the rising tide of electro-magnetic pollution in the environment.

This book is an updated version of Alanna Moore's 'Divining Earth Spirit' (published 1994), which evolved out of her own geomantic insights and interviews, and the information gathered in her various dowsing and geomancy magazines over 20 years.

Permaculture in Action by Alanna Moore

Permaculture is a design system for sustainable homes, farms, gardens and communities that was developed in Australia over 20 years ago by Bill Mollison and David Holmgren. Most books on permaculture have been mainly theoretical. Now here is a book which is showcasing gems of permaculture design, as well as revealing the people behind them, their inspirations and motivations.

Alanna Moore has been studying, practising and teaching permaculture since 1987. She has been involved with writing for and helping produce two permaculture magazines since 1991 - the Permaculture International Journal and Green Connections. Alanna has been a roving reporter, travelling around Australia gathering stories and photos of permaculture people, places and innovations.

This book is a collection of these stories, with many new ones not published in Australia before. Alanna, who now writes for Acres USA, documents the power of people, who, with a good plan, have overcome land degradation, thereby promoting the sustainable productivity of Mother Earth, while working in harmony with nature.

Both books will be published sometime in 2001. Contact:
Python Press, PO Box 929, Castlemaine, Vic. 3450, Australia.